ON THE RUFFSTUFF

Cycling in Dalby Forest near Staindale Lake

ON THE RUFFSTUFF

84 Bike Rides in Northern England

by

J. BRIAN BEADLE

CICERONE PRESS
MILNTHORPE, CUMBRIA

© J. Brian Beadle 1995
ISBN 1 85284 190 7
A catalogue record for this book is available from the British Library.

DEDICATION

*To my sons Jonathan and Christopher for taking me along some
of the most ferocious downhill tracks in Yorkshire and
not laughing at my aerobatics!*

ADVICE TO READERS

Readers are advised that whilst every effort is taken by the author
to ensure the accuracy of this guidebook, changes can occur which
may affect the contents. A book of this nature is more prone to
change than a more general guide. It is advisable to check locally on
transport, accommodation, shops, etc.

The publisher would welcome notes of any changes.

Front Cover: Struggling up the Middleton Incline on the High Peak Trail

CONTENTS

Chapter 4 - West & South Yorkshire

Chapter 5 - North Humberside

Chapter 6 - Nottinghamshire

Chapter 7 - The Yorkshire Dales

Chapter 8 - The Trans Pennine Trail

Chapter 9 - Cumbria

Chapter 10 - Cheshire & Lancashire

Chapter 11 - South Tyneside & Northumberland

PREFACE

Resting alongside Lilla Cross on the North York Moors one balmy summer's afternoon after an exhilarating ride across Fylingdales Moor gave me the inspiration to write this book. The sheer beauty of the purple heather clad moor, the solitude and the views make this my favourite place on Earth, whether in the hot summer sun or in the depths of winter with a biting north east wind. Yes, even on the high moors winter riding is a possibility if you have respect for the conditions and are correctly attired. A foray onto the moors on a crisp, frosty, sunny morning has to be one of life's better experiences. The contrast between winter and summer riding is vast, from the snow on the heather to the exquisite carpet of purple in the summer when the tracks are hard and fast.

Some of the tracks which I rode to enable me to write this book were not conquered easily. Whilst chasing my sons over some remote part of a Yorkshire moorland track I learned how to fly several times, and as I grow older, although the youthful enthusiasm is still intact and raring to go, I find that at over fifty years of age learning teenage skills comes hard, with some very hard, but may I say graceful falls only firing the enthusiasm for more punishment.

The rewards of achievement are many for all terrain cyclists. They traverse mile after mile of track to search out the wildest and most beautiful places in England, only to return home with aching limbs, covered in mud and possibly a thumping headache from the continuous pounding of a hard day's ride. Still they return time and time again to enjoy the adrenaline pumping rides which only an off road cyclist can appreciate.

Please have a regard for other users of the tracks and hail them a cheery good-day as you pass, and if you see a hardened old chap gracefully sailing over the handlebars of his Kona ATB please give him a hand up out of the mud. When you do, just look at the grin on his face as he remounts and rides off into the sunset.

I hope you enjoy yourselves as much!

J. Brian Beadle 1995

On the Scarborough to Whitby Trailway at Burniston
The author at Lilla Cross

Beamish Shorthorns on the Consett/Sunderland railway path
On the banks of Carsington Water

INTRODUCTION

Since the invention of the wheel fascination with personal transport has amused and bemused man. From Velocipede to Boneshaker and Penny Farthing to Tandem, he has devised unique ways of transporting himself efficiently, economically and speedily on our roads.

Several years ago a burst of creativity created a tough, innovative form of transport. The Mountain Bike was born. With twenty-one or more gears, an efficient braking system, a lightweight but strong frame and more recently a sophisticated suspension system. It was a go anywhere, climb anything form of transport which caught the imagination of cyclists young and old, breathing new life into tired limbs.

This book bridges the gap between social cycling, where it is safe to take the family for an afternoon's ride, and the more adventurous rider seeking tough and demanding routes on the nation's bridleways and rough tracks.

The variety of routes to be found in this book will suit all tastes with many on bridleways, hard surfaced disused railway tracks and wide forest roads where there is the option of scurrying off onto the rougher woodland tracks. All routes have a historic theme to them and many have been devised by local and county councils with attention paid to safety to give an alternative traffic-free cross-city route with a hard surface to ride on. Many are on old railway tracks bought by councils and converted for use by cyclists, horse riders and walkers. Magnificent sculptures have been commissioned using natural resources along some of the routes and picnic places provided to give riders a welcome stopping place to rest their weary limbs.

You will find that the accent of most of these graded routes is cycling for pleasure and many historical features are pointed out as well as places to take refreshment along the way.

The routes through County Durham are mainly on disused railway tracks which are purpose built for the cyclist, weaving their way through the Land of the Prince Bishops. Derbyshire is another area that has many old railway tracks, remnants of the coal mining days, which today provide safe transport through some of the finest scenery in England. In contrast, the more difficult but more rewarding climbs in the Yorkshire Dales, Cumbria and North York Moors test your aerobic and muscular abilities. Although a thrilling descent often compensates for the hard work!

Planners from many county, borough and metropolitan councils are busy opening new cycle routes all over the country. Perhaps the most ambitious is the 'Trans Pennine Trail' which connects the west coast at Southport to the east coast at Hornsea. This is a magnificent route which, when completed, will give cyclists, walkers and horse riders 150 miles (240km) of safe off road track.

The maps associated with each route are for guidance only and it is suggested that your route is planned well in advance using the appropriate Ordnance Survey map. When setting out on a ride please go well prepared and on a correctly maintained cycle. Make sure you have sufficient food and water with you, a map, compass, and extra clothing. A puncture outfit and a set of plastic tyre levers are essential if you are not to be stranded miles from civilisation, and don't forget the all important whistle in case you are immobilised. The international distress signal is six long whistle blasts repeated at one minute intervals. If setting out over the wilder routes it is always advisable to let someone know where you are going and your estimated time of return.

A word of warning! Please keep to recognised tracks, bridleways etc. and give way to walkers. Under no circumstances use a public footpath or open land to cycle on.

I sincerely hope that you enjoy this book and take it with you wherever you travel in the north of England, and most of all enjoy your cycling in the relative safety of a traffic-free environment.

SUSTRANS

Sustrans is short for Sustainable Transport and is a charity who design and build traffic free paths for cyclists and walkers. They try to encourage a change in transport policies as Britain tends to favour motorised transport instead of pollution free cycling. Many European countries have extensive traffic free routes for cyclists and visitors to Britain are amazed at our lack of off road facilities.

Sustrans in co-operation with local conservationists, County and Local Councils and The Countryside Commission, to mention just a few, are opening cycleways all over the country called Linear Parks, and today has over 250 miles of traffic free tracks available. Sustrans is now working towards a linked national network of these Greenways from Inverness to Dover, from London to Wales and twice across the Pennines. A feature of some of these cycleways are the Sculpture Trails, commissioned sculptures using available materials along the route. They use mileposts as works of art, a herd of cows sculpted from scrap metal called the Beamish Shorthorns grazing alongside the Consett and Sunderland Railway Path along with the Jolly Drovers Maze and massive Transformers. Many of the tracks featured are on the routes of long gone railway lines and now used for practical transport in and out of some of our cities. In the northern area the aim is to connect east and west with a cycle track from coast to coast. Eventually, a track from Inverness to the south coast is hoped for, with branches taking you into Wales and the West Country.

Sustrans can be supported by subscription. If you would like to join them they can be contacted at Sustrans, 35 King Street, Bristol BS1 4DZ.

KEY TO MAPS

●   VILLAGE OR TOWN

– – – – – –   OFF ROAD TRACK OR BRIDLEWAY

············   OTHER TRACK

————   ROAD

———→   ROUTE DIRECTION

～～～   RIVER OR STREAM

CHAPTER 1

North Yorkshire

RIDE 1: BEADLAM - BRANSDALE - RUDLAND RIGG - HUTTON LE HOLE

Fact File

Distance: 33 miles (53km)

Grading: Rough & Tough

Off Road: 38%

Start Grid Ref: Beadlam on the A170. OS Landranger 100/ 655846

Refreshments: Pubs at Gillamoor and Beadlam. At Hutton le Hole there are numerous cafes and pubs. Kirkbymoorside, cafes and pubs.

Along the Way: Views across Farndale to Blakey Ridge and Hutton Ridge. Prehistoric caves at Kirkdale and a tiny church with a fine Saxon sundial.

History: Kirkdale caves are in the cliff face just before the ford across the road. They date back to pre-historic times and are said to have been used by hyenas as a den. Bones of elephant, rhinoceros, hippopotamus and ox have been found there. The cave entrance is a narrow opening in the rock face but extends 300 feet inside the cliff. The caves were probably used when The Great Lake was in existence, making them easy to reach.

St Gregory's Minster, a tiny church rebuilt in Saxon times, has connections with early Christianity along the east coast. There is a well preserved Saxon sundial above the door on which the original Saxon inscription is still easily visible.

At Hutton le Hole there is a very good Museum with a rebuilt village. It is superb and well worth visiting.

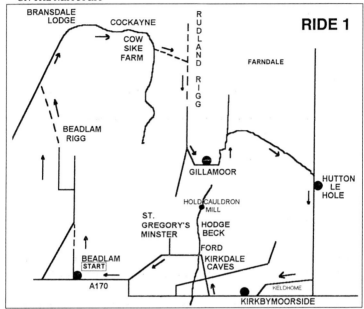

The Route

Don't be confused by the villages of Beadlam and Nawton which seem to be as one, they are so close. There is plenty of street parking in Beadlam - look out for Howl Dale Lane with the church on the corner. At the end of Howl Dale Lane take the grassy bridleway heading north along Howl Dale. This is a rough, tough, muddy track which is difficult when wet. It meets a minor road in 1 mile. Bear right here and continue along until you meet a sign for Helmsley and Pockley. Turn left here and in a couple of hundred yards turn right at the sign for Beadlam Rigg. Go straight ahead at the gate where the road becomes a wide stony track over Pockley Moor. This is wild country and can be exposed at times, but ride it in August and enjoy the purple heather clad moor. In about 3 miles the track joins the Bransdale road. Continue straight ahead and follow the road through Bransdale, then curving to the right past Bransdale Lodge and Cockayne, keeping to the main road all the way. As the road turns back along the other side of the valley watch out for a farm on the right, marked as Cow Sike Farm on the map. Ignore the bridleway sign on the left just before the farm and take the wide track opposite the farm entrance up the hill. One mile further on the track meets another track on top of Rudland Rigg.

Turn right here and enjoy a thrilling 4 mile downhill thrash towards Gillamoor. If you have time, stop to enjoy the scenery into Farndale and across to the old ironstone workings dotted all around the area.

At the road keep straight ahead, eventually taking the left fork into Gillamoor where there is a good pub. Suitably refreshed (or inebriated), keep the pub on your right and head off towards Farndale. If you haven't fallen off at the first sharp bend at the top of the steep hill which now confronts you, stop and soak up the view! At the bottom of the hill keep to the right towards Hutton le Hole, ignoring all turnings off. Turn right at the 'T' junction and thrash downhill into Hutton le Hole. You might like to visit the excellent Rural Museum here, not to be missed! There are numerous pubs and cafes and you must try the delicious homemade ice cream.

Take the Kirkbymoorside road out of the village and a few yards before the 'T' junction turn right through Keldhome on the old main road past a pretty stream. At the main road turn right again into Kirkbymoorside. Unless facilities are required in Kirkbymoorside keep straight on at the roundabout towards Helmsley. In 1 mile, just after the speed limit signs, turn right. Take care here as there is no signpost but the junction is obvious. At the crossroads keep straight ahead and soon you arrive at the top of a short, but steep hill. On the right through the trees is a cliff face where the Kirkdale Cave entrances are situated. If you want a better view go down the hill and enter the wood just before the ford. In wet weather the ford can be a raging torrent but in summer it is usually dry, as is Hodge Beck. Further upstream, at Hold Cauldron Mill, the river bed is porous and the water travels subterranean for a mile or so, unless of course it is in flood when it pours along its overland bed to deluge the road.

Carry on up the hill on the opposite side of the beck where half way up there is a sign to the right for St Gregory's Minster a couple of hundred yards along the lane. After visiting the Minster return to the road and continue up the hill which joins the main road back to Beadlam.

View along the Hambleton Drove Road

RIDE 2: HAMBLETON DROVE ROAD - HAWNBY

Fact File

Distance:	16 miles (26km)
Grading:	Moderate
Off Road:	70%
Start Grid Ref:	Car park on Hawnby to Osmotherley road. OS Landranger 100/480959
Refreshments:	None

Along the Way: The views are outstanding from the Drove Road. On a clear day the Pennines are visible and all around are pretty villages nestling in the valleys beneath tree covered hillsides.

History: The Hambleton Drove Road is an ancient highway which was used to drive cattle from the north to the south, reaching a peak in the 18th and 19th centuries. Records show that drovers

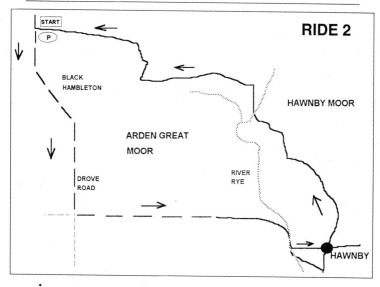

RIDE 2

START
P
BLACK HAMBLETON
ARDEN GREAT MOOR
DROVE ROAD
HAWNBY MOOR
RIVER RYE
HAWNBY

were in operation in the 14th century, but they probably relied more on cattle thieving than genuine trade in those days.

The drovers were well looked after by the inhabitants of farmsteads and hostelries along the way, alas more than we will be for the inns have been either knocked down or turned into private houses.

The Route

Start from the small car park at the side of the road and immediately join the Hambleton Drove Road going south. This climbs quite steeply to reach the highest point of the ride at Black Hambleton which is over 1200ft above sea level, and you'll know it! Continue along the wide track for 6½ miles to meet the Kepwick to Hawnby track/road. Turn left here towards Hawnby and continue on past Arden Hall to Hawnby village. Turn left in Hawnby, signposted to Osmotherley, following the undulating narrow road back to the starting point amidst beautiful wild countryside.

RIDE 3: SCARBOROUGH TO WHITBY TRAILWAY

Fact File

Distance: 20 miles (32km) 40 miles return

Grading: Easy

Off Road: 95%

Start Grid Ref: Scalby village. OS Landranger 101/015906

Refreshments: Hayburn Wyke (Old Coaching Inn), Ravenscar (including public toilets), Robin Hoods Bay, Whitby.

Along the Way: Apart from the most devastating views along this part of the Yorkshire coast make sure you see the remains of the Alum Mines, although it does involve diverting off route and walking with your cycle. At Robin Hoods Bay there is a museum and the old houses and ginnels to explore. The Abbey and Church at Whitby are steeped in history and not far away is Fortune's smoke house where herring are turned into kippers. You must try some of these most delicious kippers from this famous Yorkshire family firm.

History:

The Scarborough to Whitby Railway was completed in 1885. It is one of the most scenic routes in Britain as it climbs from Scarborough to Ravenscar where the station is at 631ft above sea level. On leaving Ravenscar the railway track descends towards Robin Hoods Bay. The line was so steep and

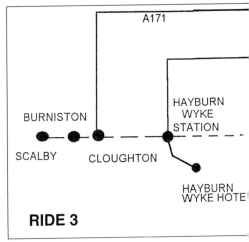

twisty that a special type of steam engine, Class W tank engine, was built for the route - it was nicknamed the 'Whitby Willie'. The line carried tourists to and from the resorts of Scarborough and Whitby but was closed in 1965.

Acknowledgement: Scarborough Borough Council

The Route
There are many access points to the railway track but the best place to start is in the country at Scalby village. Park in Station Road, Scalby and pick up the sign for The Railway Walk at the entrance to Field Close Road, following it round to the right into Lancaster Way. At the end of the street bear right to join the railway track to Burniston village. Cross the main road diagonally left at Burniston and drop down onto the track at the other side. In 1 mile at Cloughton Station, which is now a private house, pass to the left of the buildings then cross diagonally right at the road to rejoin the railway path.

Continue along for 2 miles to Hayburn Wyke Station. The railway path goes straight ahead through the gate but if refreshment is required turn right to the Hayburn Wyke Hotel, an old coaching inn.

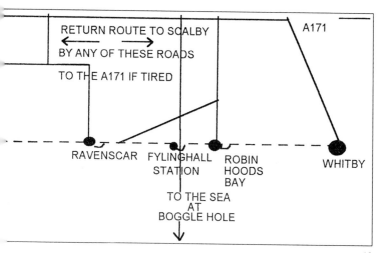

Suitably refreshed, cycle along past Staintondale Station to Ravenscar. A gentle incline upwards to a cyclist but a hard slog for a heavily laden steam engine, especially if the line is greasy with fallen leaves in the autumn. At Ravenscar you must leave the path as the tunnel which the trains used is dangerous. Turn right onto a chalky road to the square. There are a couple of houses, a shop and a cafe on one side. Keep these on your left and head north along a wide, well surfaced road to the Raven Hall Hotel.

Opposite the hotel entrance is the National Trust Centre. Take the track past the centre, following a sign for the Cleveland Way. The track soon becomes brick paved, using old bricks from the Ravenscar Brick Company; if you look carefully you can see their name on the bricks. A few yards further on where the track narrows turn left following a 'Trail' sign to rejoin the railway track. This extremely scenic route with views across to Robin Hoods Bay and beyond takes you past the old Ravenscar Brickworks; the remains of some of the kilns can still be seen. Cross the road at Fylinghall Station (you will not see the station) and continue along to Robin Hoods Bay.

Whitby Abbey. Journey's end of the Scarborough to Whitby Trailway

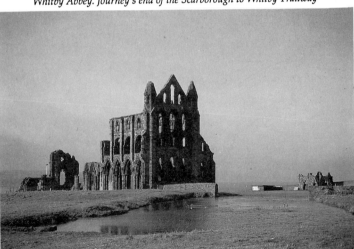

Refreshments and toilet facilities are available here in the village, but for those not requiring them simply follow the signs for the railway walk through the car park and over the road opposite to rejoin the path towards Hawsker. After crossing a caravan site road continue along the path until it meets the A171. From here take the road into Whitby to collect your Whitby Oak Smoked Kippers for tea.

RIDE 4: CLAY BANK - URRA MOOR - CLAY BANK

Fact File

Distance:	7 miles (11km)
Grading:	Moderate
Off Road:	97%
Start Grid Ref:	Clay Bank car park. OS Landranger 93/573036

Along the Way: Fantastic views to Teesside and north into County Durham from Cold Moor and south along the lush Bilsdale valley. North east from Urra Moor is the sweeping escarpment of the

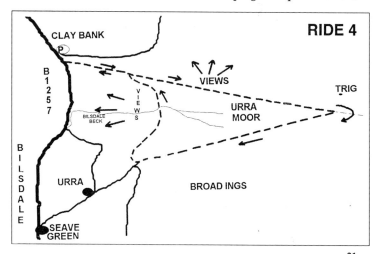

Cleveland Hills surmounted by Roseberry Topping, its peculiar shape having evolved from the mining of jet, iron ore and stone.

The Route

Please take extra care on this route as it is popular with walkers. Leave the Clay Bank car park left onto the main road uphill. In a few yards turn left at the bridleway sign up a steep climb and onto the moor. The rocky scramble ahead can be avoided by taking the track to the left. Follow the main track across Urra Moor to the high point at the Triangulation Pillar, a white marker stone on the left. Turn right down the wide track almost opposite and follow this bridleway for almost 2 miles, then leave the wide track at the corner and aim for the wall straight ahead. Just before the wall take the track to the right. Keeping the wall on your left follow the track down to a moorland beck then climb up the other side to return to the point where you came onto the moor. Take care if wet as there are many peaty bogs around; it would be a shame to lose a reader! Go left through the gate and retrace your route downhill back to the car park at Clay Bank.

RIDE 5: LANGDALE END - LANGDALE FOREST - LILLA CROSS - HARWOOD DALE

Fact File

Distance:	21 miles (33km)
Grading:	Moderate
Off Road:	70%
Start Grid Ref:	Langdale End. OS Landranger 101/939913
Refreshments:	Moorcock Inn at Langdale End. Mill Inn at Harwood Dale
Along the Way:	Lilla Cross and the views from Lilla Howe

History: Lilla Cross is said to mark the burial place of a Saxon nobleman who died saving the King's life by throwing himself on the sword of the assassin.

Acknowledgement: Forest Enterprise

The Route

There is limited parking at Langdale End. It is probably wise to park on the wide grass verge by the bridge over the River Derwent on the outskirts of the village. Leave the village past the Moorcock Inn then at the top of the hill turn right at the signpost for Birch Hall. Continue until the road forks then go right here, ignoring the Birch Hall road to the left. Soon the road becomes a track as you enter Langdale Forest. Keep straight on for about 2 miles when the road forks. Go left following the red cycle route marker. The forest road climbs for $2^{1}/_{2}$ miles to High Woof Howe; keep on the main road all the way. If in doubt bear right. At High Woof Howe the forest road bears left and downhill to exit onto the moor at the Fylingdales Early Warning Station perimeter fence.

Turn right and follow the fence on your left as the track climbs up high onto Lilla Rigg where Lilla Cross stands proud, silhouetted against the sky. Turn right at the signpost for Robin Hoods Bay, then after visiting Lilla Cross rejoin the track and head right to another signpost across the moor. Take the track to the right signed to Harwood Dale, a rough bridleway which crosses the moor over Burn Howe Rigg. In about 3 miles follow the bridleway sign into a field, keep the fence on your left, then at farm buildings cross a stile into another field on the left. Follow the fence on the left then turn right at the next field. Keep the fence on the right and head for the gate opposite for your exit. Turn immediately left and as you approach a farm turn right at the bridleway sign into the field. Follow the fence on the left to its end then take the same line to a clump of trees in the middle of the field, heading diagonally across the field to a gate opposite.

Enter the wood down the hill, turning right over the footbridge at the bottom. On reaching the field turn left and exit onto the road at Chapel Farm. Turn right at the road and meander down to the Mill Inn for some refreshment before climbing Reasty Bank. Leave the inn and continue along the road bearing right at the next junction. Keep on the main road and attack Reasty Bank. If you are lucky there might be an ice cream van waiting for you at the top!

Turn right at the crest of the hill, passing the car park, and keep right on to the forest road following the escarpment edge along to a viewpoint in a mile or so. Here you can look back over the moor

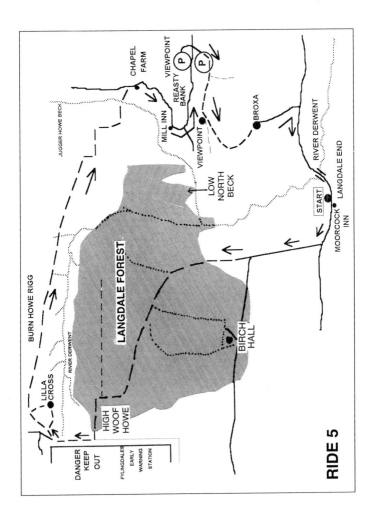

RIDE 5

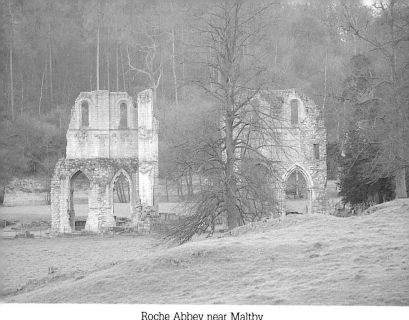

Roche Abbey near Maltby
Journey's end at Hornsea Mere

Cresswell Crags
The track over Buckden Rake

to see where you have been! Continue along the forest road without deviation to arrive at the tiny village of Broxa. Take care down the steep hill out of Broxa to the 'T' junction. Turn right here to return to Langdale End.

RIDE 6: GOATHLAND - LILLA RIGG - HORCUM - TWO HOWES RIGG

Fact File

Distance:	20 miles (32km)
Grading:	Rough & Tough
Off Road:	65%
Start Grid Ref:	Goathland. OS Outdoor Leisure 27 / Landranger 94 - 836013
Refreshments:	Goathland, pubs and cafes. Horcum car park, ice cream van in summer

Along the Way: Goathland is an interesting moorland village with the Mallyan Spout Waterfall worth visiting. The many Howes passed on the route are ancient burial grounds; there are more than 3000 on the North York Moors.

The Fylingdales Missile Tracking Station is a focal point with its pyramid radar structure now having made the 'Golf Balls' redundant. The Hole of Horcum is a massive valley scooped out of the moor by melting ice from nearby Eskdale thousands of years ago. It was the legendary home of a giant called Horcum!

The Route

Start in the village of Goathland where there is a small car park; be early as it is soon full. Head off towards Whitby then opposite the Beckhole junction, just before joining the A169, take the track through the roadside parking area on the right. At the A169 cross with care onto the moor opposite, through the gate and along the bridleway track. Just past the trees where the track splits take the more prominent one to the right to climb up to Foster Howes. Continue along past the wayside marker, Anns Cross, then a long drag over Louven Howe, keeping the fence on your right. At the

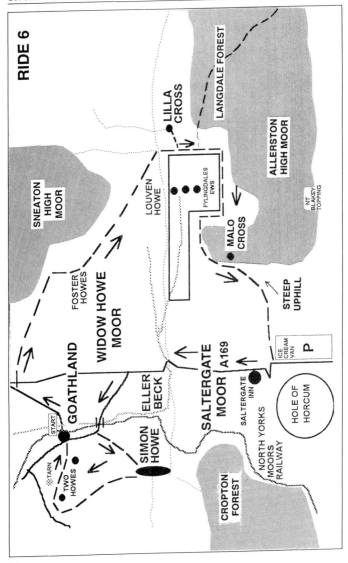

forest road turn right through the gate passing Lilla Cross on your left. (See previous ride for details of Lilla.) Continue straight ahead on the wide track parallel to the Fylingdales perimeter fence, through a gate and follow the track round to the right, still keeping close to the fence.

Eventually the track finishes at a Fylingdales access gate near the Generator House. A few yards before this at the edge of the trees go left through a small gate onto a bridleway through the heather, signed to Saltersgate & Langdale End. It is a hard slog on a rough track that eventually opens out into a field. Keep straight ahead, close to the forest on the left, to arrive at a gate and Malo Cross. Take the signed route to Horcum on the right; yes, it does go straight up the end of the rigg! If you can ride to the top without dismounting I'll buy you a pint in the Saltergate Inn - if you can catch me! At the top keep right around the edge of the escarpment, through a gate picking up the bridleway waymark, and follow these to exit carefully onto the A169, then left to the Hole of Horcum car park for your ice cream.

From the car park turn right onto the A169 and go carefully down Saltergate Hill. Refresh yourself at the Saltergate pub at the bottom of the hill and ask to see the fire that never goes out. No doubt you will be told the ghoulish reason for this; I will let you find out for yourself! Continue along past the Saltergate pub, past Fylingdales Tracking Station then down a long hill to Eller Beck; brakes on here for the nasty bend at the bottom! Half way up the other side turn left for Goathland. In 1½ miles take the bridleway left over the moor to Simon Howe. If you have had enough of rough tracks by now simply continue along the road to Goathland. For the more masochistic of you take to the moor, but be warned that it is a difficult track!

At Simon Howe take the track to the right over Two Howes Rigg. The two Howes can be seen in the distance. Keep to the left of the Howes down a sometimes difficult track downhill, past a pretty tarn to exit onto the Goathland road and return to the start.

North York Moors Forest District
A leaflet for these rides, 'Cycling in the Forest', is available from the Dalby Visitor Centre or from Forest Enterprise, 42 Eastgate, Pickering,

North Yorkshire YO18 7DU. The publication *North Riding Forest Park* is excellent for both cyclist and walker.

RIDE 7: LANGDALE FOREST

This recently planted coniferous forest was formed between 1962 and 1977. There are 4500 hectares to explore, giving cyclists scope to test all their skills. The highest point in the north at High Woof Howe is 280 metres from where some stupendous views are available. Although most cyclists will want to follow the waymarked routes there is a choice of other tracks for the more adventurous rider. As Langdale has been designated a cyclist's forest, finding and navigating new routes can be rewarding.

Forest Enterprise have provided three waymarked routes of varying difficulty. Follow signs for 'Mountain Bike Trails' from the start of the forest drive at Bickley.

Langdale Forest has many cycle tracks

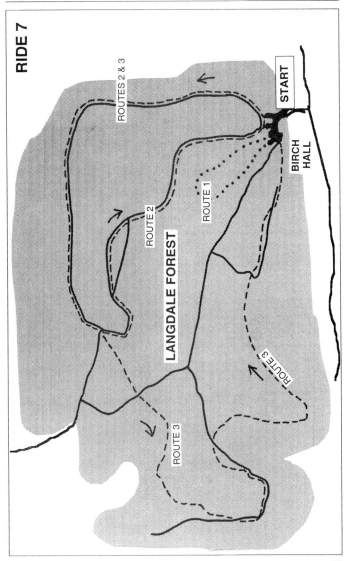

RIDE 7

START

BIRCH HALL

ROUTES 2 & 3

ROUTE 2

ROUTE 1

ROUTE 3

ROUTE 3

LANGDALE FOREST

Route 1   at 4 miles (6¹/₂km) is a gentle beginner's route but it can be tricky on the downhill grassy sections if wet.

Route 2   at 8 miles (13km) is rather more testing, starting with a long slippery climb if wet. It uses a mixture of forest roads and rough paths.

Route 3   is the one to test your mountain biking skills to the full using a lot of off road tracks with testing uphill sections followed by some tremendous downhill bashes. Once again, they can be rough and boggy in places. Suggested time is 2 hours but expert riders can see it off in less. Distance 15 miles (24km).

RIDE 8: BOLTBY FOREST

Boltby is about 5 miles north-east of Thirsk close to the Hambleton Hills. It covers 500 hectares of recently established conifer woodland planted around 1929. It overlooks the Vale of York and offers marvellous views from its high vantage point. It is difficult terrain with many steep hills and valleys which present a challenge to even the most experienced off roader. All the routes offered start from High Paradise Farm to which access is gained along the old Hambleton road from the Hawnby to Boltby road. The forest will be closed on days of pheasant shoots which will be displayed at the start at High Paradise Farm. The routes mainly follow the course of the 'Boltby Bash' competition but are not very long.

Route 1   is a short route of about 4 miles (6.5km). It is an easy route for beginners and takes about 30 minutes.

Route 2   is more testing with some good climbs and descents and takes about three-quarters of an hour for its 7 miles (11km).

Route 3   of 12 miles (19.5km) is the one for the more experienced rider and takes around an hour or more to complete depending on skills.

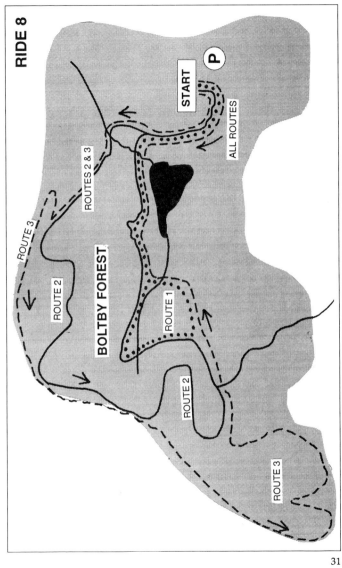

RIDE 8

P

START

ALL ROUTES

ROUTES 2 & 3

ROUTE 3

ROUTE 2

BOLTBY FOREST

ROUTE 1

ROUTE 2

ROUTE 3

RIDE 9: GUISBOROUGH FOREST

Guisborough Forest is set at the northern end of the North York Moors on the outskirts of the town of Guisborough and covers 460 hectares. Half of the forest is leasehold and cyclists may only use bridlepaths in this area. The waymarked rides are being developed in the western freehold area. The forest is used by horse riders and walkers and riders are advised to keep to the waymarked cycle routes to avoid conflict. Forest Enterprise is developing cycle routes and any new routes not in this book can be picked up at the start area at the Cleveland County Council's car park at Pinchinthorpe Station on the Guisborough walkway.

The Route
This is a fairly demanding route of around 5 miles (8.4km) and will take about 25 minutes. There are some steep climbs and descents.

RIDE 10: DALBY FOREST

Facilities for the public are numerous in the huge Dalby Forest complex and it is another forest which is designated as part of the North Riding Forest Park. There are ten car parks, several toilet blocks, an information centre and a cafe. Unfortunately there are few cycle tracks but they are able to supply advice and leaflets on tracks in other forests to supplement the ones in this book.

Route 1
This circular 8 mile (13km) route starts from the car park and information centre at Low Dalby. Take the Forest Drive road towards Bickley. En route you may like to linger a while at the lake at Low Staindale but if not follow the road past the lake, then sharp right up the hill to Adderstone Rigg. In a mile or so, at a crossroads, the Forest Drive road turns left. You must turn sharp right round the radio mast; this will take you onto a good downhill thrash back to Low Dalby.

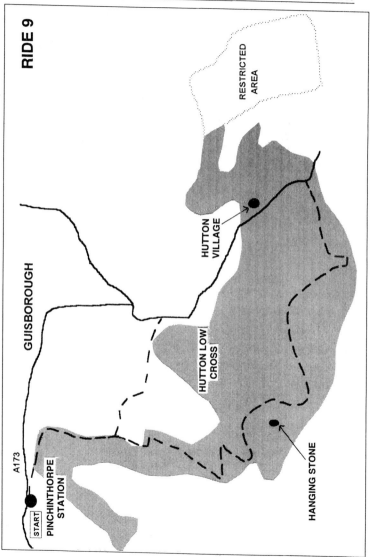

RIDE 9

GUISBOROUGH

A173

START

PINCHINTHORPE
STATION

HUTTON LOW
CROSS

HUTTON
VILLAGE

RESTRICTED
AREA

HANGING STONE

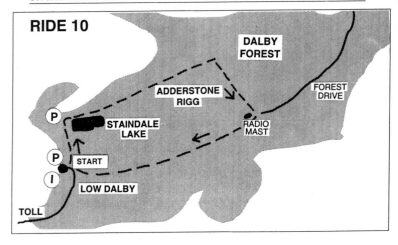

Route 2 - 18 or 36 miles (29 or 58km)

There is a longer route to consider which takes in three forests, although it is not a circular route and you must decide which way you are going to ride it. If you decide to do the return trip you will find it invigorating but tiring, for 36 miles off road does rather sap your strength.

Start at Low Dalby and follow the signs for the Forest Drive towards Bickley but this time follow it to the end. Soon you will see posts with a black cycle against a white background. This waymarks the route. Follow them until you exit the forest at Bickley and at the road 'T' junction turn left and follow the sign for Mountain Bike Trails and the waymarks for a mile or so until they direct you right into Langdale Forest at School Farm.

In about half a mile at the junction sweep round to the left following the waymark but ignoring the sign for Mountain Bike Trails. Keep following the black cycle waymark at every junction to climb up now to High Woof Howe, where at last a short downhill section leads to the Fylingdales Tracking Station fence. Leave the forest here and turn right, keeping the fence on your left.

Cross over Fylingdales Moor. On the right is Lilla Howe which is surmounted by Lilla Cross, a memorial to a brave Saxon nobleman. The views from this point are breathtaking. If you wish to visit Lilla

Cross you will have to make a slight detour.

Enter Sneaton Forest at the gate and keep following the waymarks through the forest and eventually down to the picnic place of May Beck. After perhaps soaking your feet in the cooling waters of the beck and enjoying a refreshing ice cream leave May Beck for your return journey along the same track back to Low Dalby. Or did you remember to arrange for your transport to meet you here?

RIDE 11: THE CITY OF YORK
ROWNTREES - FOSS ISLANDS - OSBALDWICK
York was Britain's No 1 cycling city in 1992.

Fact File

Distance:	3 miles (4.7km)
Grading:	Easy
Off Road:	100%
Start Grid Ref:	Wigginton Road, York. OS Landranger 105/ 603535

Along the Way: Pipework sculptures and carved seating

History: Part of the Derwent Valley Light Railway track is used for this short city crossing. It provides a quick traffic-free route traversing the City of York from the Rowntrees factory on the Wigginton Road to Metcalfe Lane at Osbaldwick.

Acknowledgements: Sustrans & York City Council

The Route

This route is described as a Linear Nature Park. It runs from the Wigginton Road near Rowntrees (now Nestlé) chocolate factory in York to Metcalfe Lane at Osbaldwick. It uses the old railway line and is 3 miles in length. Work on the track started in 1992 and it is being constantly improved. Sculptures have been commissioned along the route as well as the carving of seats. It should prove very popular with the residents of this cycling City of York for cross-city transport.

HARROGATE - YORK

Fact File

Distance:	3 miles (5km)
Grading:	Easy
Off Road:	100%
Start Grid Ref:	Spofforth. OS Landranger 104/365507
Refreshments:	Pubs and cafes at Wetherby. Pub at Spofforth
Acknowledgement:	Sustrans, Harrogate Borough Council

The Route

This cycle path is only at stage one, the length completed being from Spofforth to Wetherby. Future extensions to reach Harrogate and York are planned using bridleways and quiet country roads.

RIDE 12: YORK-SELBY CYCLE ROUTE

Fact File

Distance:	15 miles (24km)
Grading:	Easy
Off Road:	100%
Start Grid Ref:	Acaster Bridge access. OS Landranger 105/590474

History: The cycle track uses the old York to Selby railway line which was closed in 1983. Sustrans bought the track north of Riccall to Selby and the cycle path was opened in 1987.

Acknowledgement: Sustrans

The Route

The cycle path links up with the York to Beningbrough cycle path via a riverside path, adding an extra stretch to the route at the northern end. Access is gained to the railway track at Acaster Bridge at Bishopthorpe linking up with a route via normal roads if you wish to start in the city. The Selby to Howden link is expected to be opened shortly (1995) as part of the Trans Pennine Trail once legal problems have been sorted out.

CHAPTER 2
County Durham

Durham County Council have produced some excellent leaflets describing these rides and thanks are appropriate to them for allowing me to reproduce some of them in this book. They are available by post, (cheques payable to Durham County Council) from the Environment Department, Durham County Council, County Hall, Durham DH1 5UQ:

Cycling in County Durham £1.95 plus 45p post & packing
Railway Walks 99p plus 75p post & packing
(Both prices correct at time of publication. Please ring Durham CC on 0191 383 4144 for price check.)

RIDE 13: BRANDON - BISHOP AUCKLAND - DEERNESS VALLEY

Fact File

Distance:	15 miles (24km)
Grading:	Easy
Off Road:	75%
Start Grid Ref:	Picnic Area on B6302. OS Landranger 88/252415
Refreshments:	Pub at Waterhouses and a cafe at Esh Winning

Along the Way: Brancepeth Castle was bought in 1796 by a Sunderland banker. His son rebuilt much of it in Norman style. There is a view across to Whitworth Hall, of Bobby Shafto fame. Ushaw College on a hill to the north is a Roman Catholic Seminary and boasts a splendid Victorian chapel. On the opposite side of the valley from the Deerness line is Sleetburn Mill and Bleach Green Farm; both were involved in the processing of cloth.

History: Both lines were built to carry coal. The Deerness valley line existed for 93 years from 1858.

Acknowledgement: Durham County Council

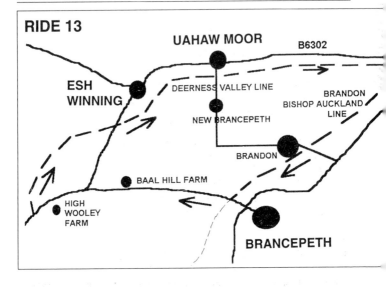

RIDE 13

UAHAW MOOR

B6302

ESH
WINNING

DEERNESS VALLEY LINE

BRANDON
BISHOP AUCKLAND
LINE

NEW BRANCEPETH

BRANDON

BAAL HILL FARM

HIGH
WOOLEY
FARM

BRANCEPETH

Brancepeth Castle near Durham

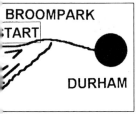

BROOMPARK

START

DURHAM

The Route
Start at the Broompark picnic area on the B6302 about a mile from Stonebridge. Follow the sign for 'Railway Walks', turning left at the track then shortly right to join the Brandon - Bishop Auckland railway track. After negotiating a deep valley, pass behind Langley Moor and Meadowfield taking a detour around the cricket field. The railway track now leads to Brancepeth Station and turns right onto the quiet Wolsingham road. In 2¹/₂ miles pass Baal Hill Farm on the right, then at the junction cross over the road passing High Wooley Farm on the left.

Shortly, down the hill turn right at the power lines through gates to a steep forest track. This is the old Waggonway to Hamilton Row and Waterhouses. Take the Deerness Walk track behind the Black Horse pub for your return route to the Broompark picnic area.

RIDE 14: LANCHESTER VALLEY - DEERNESS VALLEY

Fact File

Distance:	15 miles (24km)
Grading:	Easy
Off Road:	50%
Start Grid Ref:	Picnic area on B6302. OS Landranger 88/252415
Refreshments:	Lanchester, pubs and cafes
Along the Way:	Remains of monk's retreat at Beaurepair
History:	Both railway lines were built to carry coal
Acknowledgement:	Durham County Council

The Route
Leave the Broompark picnic area following signs for the Lanchester Valley Walk on the left. Pass under Relly Mill Bridge then accompany the railway for a while. In 1¹/₂ miles the track crosses the road to

Bearpark and the remains of the old colliery. Why not visit the ruins of Beaurepair from which Bearpark takes its name? It is where the monks came to rest in the country especially at harvest time.

The route now takes you to Langley Park and thereafter becomes wooded and on to the Malton picnic area by the River Browney before hurtling along to Lanchester, where refreshment is available if required. At Lanchester, which is named after a Roman fort, turn left where the road crosses the railway path and in about 50 yards take the left fork to join the B6301 Ford road. Uphill now for 3 miles to the summit at Wilks Hill; stop and enjoy the superb view! Turning left at the crossroads takes you to Quebec then right just after the Hamsteels Inn down a steep hill. Take the B6302 left at the bottom of the hill to Esh Winning and at the Stags Head go straight across into Station Avenue. The road curves left; look carefully for a gap in the fence leading to the Deerness Valley Railway Walk. Turn left towards Durham and follow the River Deerness for 3 miles to the Broompark picnic area.

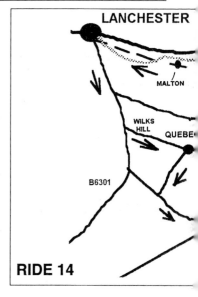

RIDE 14

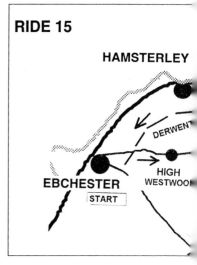

RIDE 15

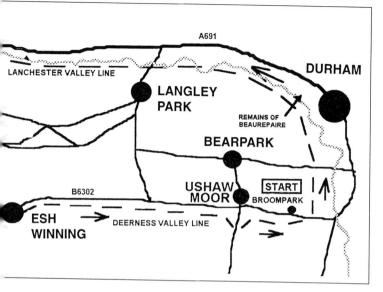

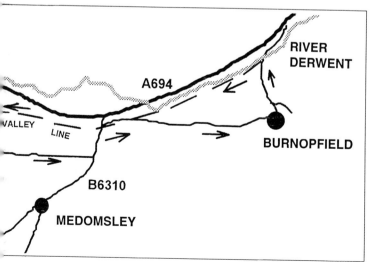

RIDE 15: DERWENT WALK - BURNOPFIELD - LEAP MILL FARM

Fact File

Distance:	15 miles (24km)
Grading:	Easy
Off Road:	60%
Start Grid Ref:	Ebchester. OS Landranger 88/106548
Refreshments:	Leap Mill Farm (Sundays in summer)

Along the Way: Leap Mill Farm 18th-century watermill, Derwenthaugh Coke Works, ruins of Gibside Hall, Derwentcote Steel Furnace, Ebchester Museum (key available from Mains Farm).

History: The Derwent Valley Railway was opened in 1867 with six stations. It carried passengers, timber, bricks and coal. Iron ore was taken to the steelworks at Consett. The line closed in 1962.

Acknowledgement: Durham County Council

The Route

The route uses quiet roads to rejoin the eastern end of the Derwent Walk, returning on this old railway track to the starting point at the car park near Ebchester.

Starting at the car park near the Derwent Walk pub head north along the Derwent Walk track then east and in 1¹/₂ miles turn right onto a tarmac road leading to High Westwood. Turn left, enjoying views of the Derwent valley, continuing for 1¹/₂ miles until you meet the B6310. Turn left again and head in the direction of Burnopfield. In Burnopfield turn left at the old Co-op store down Busty Bank to Leap Mill Farm on the left at the bottom of the hill. Turn right onto the B6314 travelling downhill towards the River Derwent. Just before the stone bridge turn left along a track that leads back to the Derwent Walk. Heading west along the disused railway track takes you back to the start at Ebchester.

RIDE 16: AUCKLAND WALK - BRANDON - BISHOP AUCKLAND

Fact File

Distance:	18 miles (29km)
Grading:	Easy
Off Road:	Route 1 - 90%. Route 2 - 90%
Start Grid Ref:	Spennymoor. OS Landranger 93/245337
Refreshments:	Bishop Auckland

Along the Way: Newton Cap Viaduct, Bishop Auckland, Auckland Castle, Binchester Roman Fort (Route 2), Brancepeth Castle although medieval it was bought by a Sunderland banker whose son rebuilt much of the castle in the Norman style with chessmen-like towers, Whitworth Hall (once the home of Bobby Shafto).

History: The line carried coal and coke in its heyday and was conceived by George Hudson.

Acknowledgement: Durham County Council

Route 1

Start at the Whitworth Road car park in Spennymoor and follow the Auckland Walk route towards Bishop Auckland. In about a mile, just past the stone cottages at Old Park Terrace, take the narrow track to the left staying with the Auckland Walk. Cross the road at the old Byers Green Railway Station; this is now a picnic area with views across the Wear Valley. Continue on the Auckland Walk track until you reach the outskirts of Bishop Auckland. A sign near the tunnel proclaims 'Bishop Auckland 1 mile'. In 100 yards go right along a path up the embankment onto the A689. Turn left down a steep hill then climb up to a sign 'Castle Chare' which will take you into the market place. Note the residence of the Bishop of Durham, Durham Castle, on the right. *(Route 2 users join here.)* Follow the one way system around the church and Town Hall, bearing left into North Bondgate then climbing to the mini-roundabout at High Bondgate. Go right into Bridge Street at the Newton Cap pub. In 150

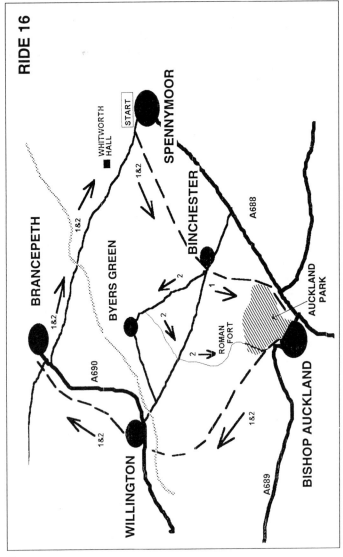

yards turn right before the terrace of houses to join the Brandon - Bishop Auckland walk track and the Newton Cap viaduct. Pass over the viaduct and in 3 miles approach Willington. Cross over the road and join the track at the other side. Beware of pedestrians! Please give way. The road through the town is accessed by a narrow path that runs to the left of a block of flats. Across the road and slightly to the right pass through the gates that lead out of town. In 2 miles turn right onto the A690 where you should turn right again. In $1/4$ mile turn left at the sign for 'Spennymoor and Page Bank'.

Enjoy the view across to Brancepeth Castle on the left and then speed down the hill to the River Wear which is the start of a 2 mile uphill slog. Watch out for the home of 'Bobby Shafto,' Whitworth Hall, as you gasp for breath up the incline. Whitworth Road car park is only a short distance from the hall.

Route 2

Follow the start instructions as for Route 1 then at the cottages at Old Park Terrace go along the narrower left fork as in Route 1 but instead of continuing on the Auckland Walk take the next turning to the right, then right again to join the Byers Green road. In a few hundred yards turn left just after Byers Green House. Cross over the next road following the signs for 'Binchester'. Follow the route downhill to the river. After passing a terrace of houses climb the hill into Bishop Auckland. Follow the instructions for Route 1 at the words 'Route 2 users join here'.

RIDE 17: CHESTER-LE-STREET - BEAMISH - CAUSEY ARCH

Fact File

Distance:	22 miles (35km)
Grading:	Easy
Off Road:	60%
Start Grid Ref:	Chester-le-Street. OS Landranger 88/273536
Refreshments:	Pubs along the way
Along the Way:	Look out for fantastic sculptures along the

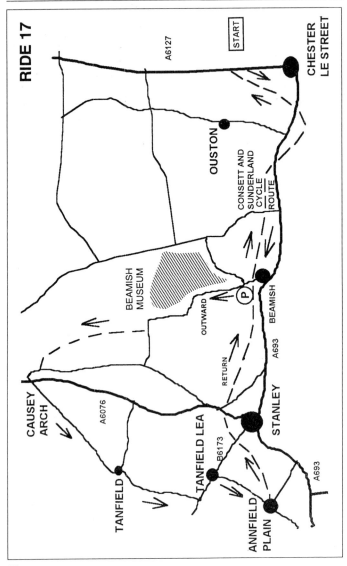

railway path. Some are made out of scrap metal to form herds of cows, whilst others are sculpted out of natural stone.

History: The old Consett to Sunderland railway track is now a cycle path created by Sustrans.

Both steam and horse drawn waggons worked the tracks carrying iron ore to the Consett steel works which gave both life and death to the railway, for the closure of the works brought about the closure of the railway and it was opened as a multi-user path in 1990.

Acknowledgements: Durham County Council, Sustrans

The Route

This route uses part of the Consett and Sunderland Railway Path following the old railway route west of Chester-le-Street.

Start at the Wheatsheaf pub which is 1¹/₂ miles north of Chester-le-Street on the A6127 where parking is available by kind permission of Bass Ltd. Go along a track between the pub and the bridge, up a ramp and onto the cycle path that crosses the east coast line on a footbridge. After 5 miles the path goes through a tunnel and you are confronted by a herd of cows. Worry not, these Beamish Shorthorns are sculpted from scrap metal by Sally Mathews!

Leave the path by a ramp on the right to the Eden Place picnic area. Go past the information board to the lower car park and bear right to join the road opposite the Shepherd & Shepherdess pub. Turn left past the golf club then uphill. Look out for the Causey Arch footpath sign and turn right here. At the top bear left through the gate, past a farm to meet the road ahead. Turn right then left at the Causey Arch Inn. Cross the A 6076 then continue on to Tanfield.

Go left downhill then first right past the 'Ever Ready' complex. In just under a mile turn left opposite the shops, then left again and right opposite the chapel into West Street. Carry straight on at the crossroads curving past the Earl Grey pub to the main road. Turn left towards Annfield Plain then left just before the Winners pub and left again in 50 yards to join the cycle path. Soon bear left and enjoy a scintillating descent of around 9 miles back to the Wheatsheaf at the start.

RIDE 18: LOW PITTINGTON - SHADFORTH - LUDWORTH

Fact File

Distance:	15 miles (24km)
Grading:	Easy
Off Road:	20%
Start Grid Ref:	Low Pittington. OS Landranger 88/327447
Refreshments:	Pubs here and there along the route

Along the Way: Views towards the Pennines are most rewarding on this ride. On the bridleways the wild flowers are in profusion in the summer months. Ludworth Tower was built in 1422 as a fortified manor house; just the ruins remain *(so much for the fortification!)*

Acknowledgement: Durham County Council

The Route

This is a very hilly area of County Durham, enjoyable because of the marvellous views but tiring on the limbs.

Start from the old signpost 'To Durham and Rainton' at Low Pittington. Go downhill then left at the Blacksmith's Arms pub heading towards the village of Sherburn. Go straight over the crossroads following the signs for Bowburn and the A1(M). The quiet country road leads you towards Bowburn. At the bottom of the hill pass under the motorway and turn left at the sign for Old Quarrington. Go straight ahead now, passing a stone house on the left then right past the farm buildings at the end of the tarmac road.

At Home Farm House on the right continue along uphill on the rough track and through a gate to join the quarry road. Turning right onto the quarry road watch out for the bridleway on the right before the quarry entrance. In $1/2$ mile leave the track onto the Quarrington Hill road. Turn left at the old church and descend steeply downhill with caution, turning right at the single track road blue sign at the bottom of the hill. Total effort is required now to climb to the top to Old Cassop. Go down the narrow road past the farm then turn left onto the A181 Durham road. In $1/2$ mile turn right

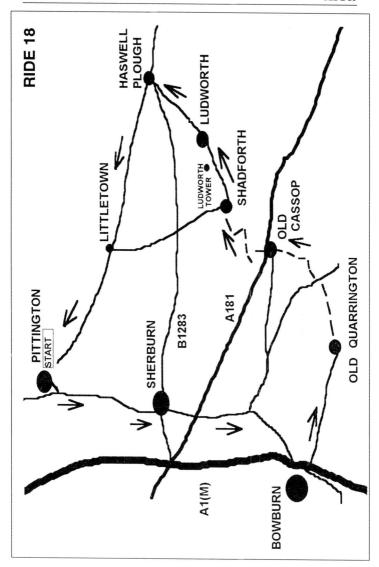

RIDE 18

PITTINGTON
START

HASWELL PLOUGH

LITTLETOWN

LUDWORTH

LUDWORTH TOWER

SHADFORTH

OLD CASSOP

SHERBURN

B1283

A181

OLD QUARRINGTON

A1(M)

BOWBURN

near the garage onto the bridleway alongside the buildings. Fork left at the quarry gates that lead to Shadforth village green and continue on to Ludworth, passing Ludworth Tower on the left. At the village turn left towards Haswell Plough, then left again at the main road and in $1/2$ mile right to join a small road passing Haswell Moor Farm. It is not far now to Littletown then back to the start at Low Pittington.

RIDE 19: THE WASKERLEY WAY

Fact File

Distance:	10 miles (16km)
Grading:	Moderate +
Off Road:	100%
Start Grid Ref:	Near Castleside. OS Landranger 88/099493

Along the Way: There are many features of the railway on this route. Hownes Gill Viaduct is 150ft high and replaced a lift system and later a funicular. There are inclines and deep cuttings on the route that were built with hard labour using picks, shovels and muscle! Waskerley village was the centre of activity during the life of the railway, supporting a large community at 1150ft above sea level.

History: The Waskerley Way is on the western part of the railway built to carry iron from Weardale to South Shields. Unfortunately the owners only had a lease on the land and the high rent was one of the reasons for the company's bankruptcy in 1840.

Acknowledgement: Durham County Council

The Route
Start near the Hownes Gill Viaduct at Castleside. The track then heads off through Rowley Station, which was dismantled and rebuilt at the Beamish Museum, then continues past the Whitehall picnic area near Nanny Mayor's Incline. Nanny Mayor was an alehouse keeper alongside the track. The incline was used until 1859 when a diversion was made via Burnhill Junction where you must

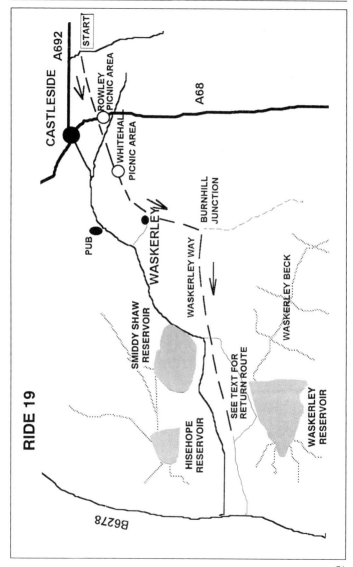

RIDE 19

CASTLESIDE   A692

START

ROWLEY PICNIC AREA

WHITEHALL PICNIC AREA

A68

BURNHILL JUNCTION

WASKERLEY

WASKERLEY WAY

PUB

SMIDDY SHAW RESERVOIR

HISEHOPE RESERVOIR

SEE TEXT FOR RETURN ROUTE

WASKERLEY BECK

WASKERLEY RESERVOIR

B6278

turn sharp right for the track to Waskerley. Now the ride becomes tougher with a climb onto and across the exposed moor. The views make up for it, however, with three reservoirs in sight. At the high point of the moor the track levels out and continues for a further couple of miles at a white road. The choice is yours now for the return to the start. You can simply turn round and speed back the way you came, take to the road and call at the pub near the Smiddy Shaw Reservoir or take the white road to the Waskerley Reservoir then back to the railway track and retrace your route to the start. I must emphasise that the white road is **not** a right of way but the latter part is used by the public to visit the reservoir occasionally.

RIDE 20: HAMSTERLEY FOREST

This large forest in south Durham was bought by the Forestry Commission from the Surtees family in 1927 and now boasts over 2000 hectares of woodland. The original broadleaved woodland, a hay meadow and the forest are for all to explore. There is a small charge to enter the forest where there is a car park, refreshments, toilets and an information centre. An unusual feature of Hamsterley is the sculpted trees. In 1987 a huge beech tree was uprooted in the autumn storms. It was sawn into four pieces and planted upside down around a dead oak tree. Then an unusual creation took place. Sculptor Chris Sell began carving the oak tree into a seat with two windows. The beech was then carved into sun and stars to form a roof, and the trunks into birds, tea and sandwiches. At ground level are crickets and fish. The sculpture is called 'Woodhenge' and is situated at the Oak Tree Car Park on the Forest Drive not far from the information centre.

Access to Hamsterley Forest is signed from the Wolsingham to Hamsterley road and the cycle rides start from the visitor centre where it is advisable to pick up a leaflet.

Route 1
This is an easy route of 4½ miles (8km) along the Bedburn Beck valley with a fairly steep bank not far from the start. It encompasses

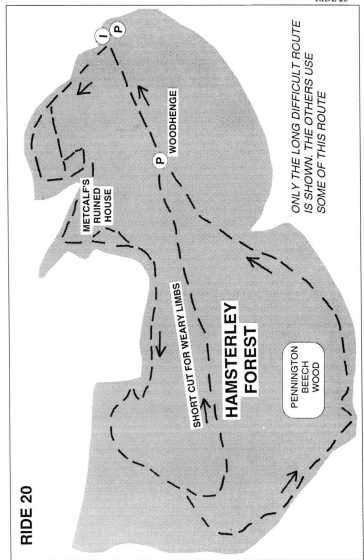

RIDE 20

ONLY THE LONG DIFFICULT ROUTE
IS SHOWN. THE OTHERS USE
SOME OF THIS ROUTE

WOODHENGE

METCALF'S
RUINED
HOUSE

SHORT CUT FOR WEARY LIMBS

HAMSTERLEY
FOREST

PENNINGTON
BEECH
WOOD

*Many interesting features are to be found in the Hamsterley Forest.
This sculpture is an upside down tree*

the Bedburn Valley Forest Nature Reserve where a wide variety of
wildlife, trees and wild flowers can be seen.

Route 2

This is a rough and tough route if
you take to the off road sections.
It is either 7 miles (11km) or 16
miles (25km) in length as there is
a choice of different waymarked
loops taking you onto sometimes
difficult tracks through the forest.
They eventually meet up with
the forest road waymarks further
along. The trail uses a com-
bination of forest drive, forest
roads and off road tracks. It is a
very scenic route full of wildlife
which the observant rider will

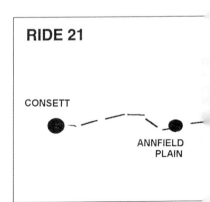

RIDE 21

CONSETT

ANNFIELD
PLAIN

54

detect. There are sparrow hawks, crossbills and curlews there for your delight.

RIDE 21: THE CONSETT AND SUNDERLAND RAILWAY PATH

Distance:	24 miles (39km)
Grading:	Easy
Off Road:	100%
Start Grid Ref:	Consett. OS Landranger 88/112507

History: The Stanhope & Tyne Railway used this track and was open from 1834 to 1985. Originally it used horse drawn waggons. In later years it carried iron ore to the huge steelworks at Consett. The closure of the works left the railway stranded and it was inevitably closed.

Along the Way: The 24 miles of cycle track abounds with bizarre sculptures, works of art for you to enjoy as you cycle past. Wonder at the two huge metal statues created from metal from old transformers, then soak up the beauty of the Kyo Undercurrent or the Jolly Drovers Maze and Forge. Or perhaps you will stop and marvel at the Beamish Shorthorns made from scrap metal.

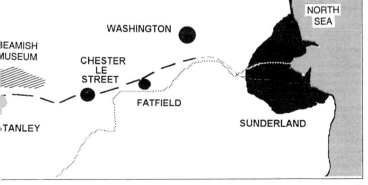

Acknowledgement: Durham County Council

The Route
There are so many access points to the track I suggest you obtain the official leaflet from Durham County Council for information, if you do not want to cycle the full length. It can be used in conjunction with other tracks to form a circular route. (See the Durham rides.)

The track deviates from the railway at various points but is well signed to bring you back onto it. The Sunderland end of the track follows existing paths through the Country Park and there is a narrow path on the Tunstall Tramway for those who have the energy left to cycle to the coast.

The colourful leaflet on the ride is available from Durham County Council at the address at the start of this chapter.

CHAPTER 3

Derbyshire & Staffordshire

DERBYSHIRE

Derbyshire County Council have produced leaflets on some of the following rides. Information is available from tourist information centres in the area and Derbyshire CC, Tel. 01629 580000. Or write to County Offices, Matlock DE4 3AG.

RIDE 22: THE HIGH PEAK TRAIL

Fact File

Distance:	17¹/₂ miles (27¹/₂km)
Grading:	Easy
Off Road:	100%
Start Grid Ref:	High Peak Junction. OS Outdoor Leisure 24/314559
Refreshments:	Picnic sites are provided along the route

Along the Way: There are many interesting features to see along the trail. Stop at the Black Rocks where there is a picnic area and toilets. Linger a while at Middleton Top and visit the Engine House where the old steam engine still remains and is open to the public at weekends during the summer months. There are the old railway buildings at High Peak Junction and the Cromford Canal to explore, although there is no cycling allowed alongside the canal.

At Cromford, Arkwrights Mill is worthy of a look to see the old buildings crumbling away. It is progressively being restored and many of the old mill's features still remain. There are various craft shops and a cafe if you wish to visit them.

Other points of interest are the Harboro Rocks, Hopton Tunnel, and the inclines at Hopton, Middleton and at Sheep Pasture. If cycling down the inclines, beware! Your speed can build up quickly. If cycling up the inclines I hope you are fit!

History:
Severe engineering difficulties prevented the building of a canal over the 1000ft limestone plateau of the Peak District so the canal engineers turned their hand to building a

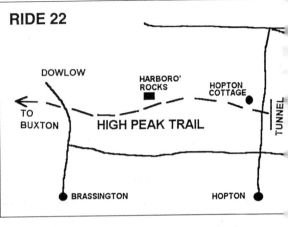

railway line instead. It was built on canal building principles but using steep inclines instead of locks to gain height. The engines were hauled up the inclines by stationary steam engines that winched the carriages up the steep slope. In 1830 the 33 mile Cromford and High Peak Railway was opened to provide a link

Top of the incline at Middleton Top. High Peak Trail

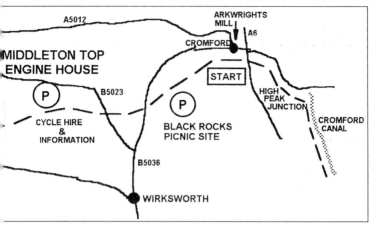

from the Cromford Canal to the Peak Forest Canal at Whaley Bridge. The line was built by Josiah Jessop, son of the builder of the Cromford Canal. During its life it was used to haul limestone, lime, coal, agricultural products and occasionally people. As the national railway system expanded it gradually put the Cromford to High Peak Railway out of business and in 1853 it was only used as a branch line for local requirements until its closure in 1967.

The railway track was bought by the Derbyshire County Council and The Peak Park Planning Board to be used for recreational purposes, thus giving birth to the High Peak Trail.

Acknowledgement: Peak National Park Authority, Derbyshire CC

The Route
The 17¹/₂ mile High Peak Trail runs from the High Peak Junction near Cromford and crosses the limestone plateau to Dowlow near Buxton. Riding the trail is a simple matter of following the signs. It is a haven of wildlife with lapwings, skylarks and curlews in prominence. The whole route is a refuge for flora and sections are designated as Nature Reserves by the Derbyshire Wildlife Trust. The limestone of the district was formed millions of years ago when the land was under water. The rock is now used for dry stone walls and many buildings along the way. Enjoy the High Peak Trail and spend time to stop off at the various places of historical interest.

RIDE 23: THE TISSINGTON TRAIL

Fact File

Distance:	13 miles (21km)
Grading:	Easy
Off Road:	100%
Start Grid Ref:	Mapleton Lane Ashbourne. OS Landranger 128/176470
Refreshments:	There are lots of picnic areas on the route
Along the Way:	Tissington village with its Wells is worth exploring

History: The Tissington Trail uses part of the disused Ashbourne to Buxton railway track. It was opened in 1899 for traffic but was never much of a success, carrying milk to the towns and limestone from quarries to the kilns near Buxton. The line was partially closed in 1963 and finally in 1967.

Acknowledgement: Peak National Park Authority, Derbyshire CC

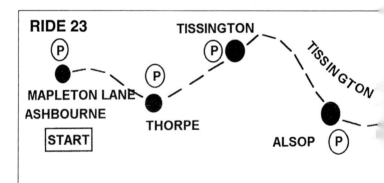

The Route

Like the High Peak Trail the Tissington Trail is owned by Derbyshire County Council and the Peak National Park Authority. It runs for 13 miles from Mapleton Lane at Ashbourne to join the High Peak Trail at Parsley Hay. The best way to locate the start is to follow the signs for the Tissington Trail from Ashbourne market place. There is a host of wildlife to be seen along the way and the trail is a joy for nature lovers. There are many picnic sites to be found and some of the old railway buildings are used as recreational buildings, whilst the old signal box at Hartington is now an information centre. You may see a dew pond or come across some of the old limekilns as you cycle along. Whatever you find you will enjoy the ride from this vantage point in the Peak District.

RIDE 24: THE MONSAL TRAIL

Fact File

Distance:	$2^{1}/_{2}$ miles (4km)
Grading:	Easy
Off Road:	100%
Start Grid Ref:	Bakewell Station. OS Outdoor Leisure 24/223690

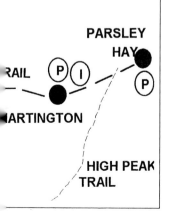

Refreshments: Bakewell

History: The Monsal Trail was born from the closure of the former Midland Railway line that passed through the Peak National Park. The line was used for the transportation of milk, coal and passengers but in the 1950s the line started to decline. Eventual closure came about in 1968. Twelve years later the Peak National Park Authority purchased the land and formed the Monsal Trail.

Acknowledgement: Peak National

Park Authority, Derbyshire CC

The Route
The Monsal Trail is 8¹/₂ miles long but cyclists are restricted to a section of only 2¹/₂ miles from Bakewell Station to Longstone. The trail is littered with mills, limekilns, old buildings and even a viaduct. Alas, most of the interesting features are at the northern end of the trail and are not available to cyclists. It is worth taking the road from Longstone to the viewpoint at Monsal Head. The scenery from this high vantage point is absolutely superb, looking along Monsal Dale which is the route of the River Wye. Hopefully one day the trail along this beautiful valley will be opened up for cyclists to enjoy.

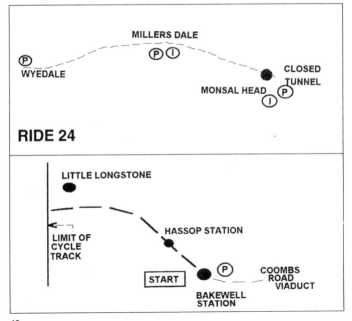

RIDE 25: THE SETT VALLEY TRAIL

Fact File

Distance:	2¹/₂ miles (4km)
Grading:	Easy
Off Road:	100%
Start Grid Ref:	Hayfield. OS Outdoor Leisure 1/036869
Refreshments:	None

History: The Hayfield Railway Line was opened in 1868 to accommodate the transportation of coal, raw materials and finished goods to and from mills in the Sett valley. It also carried a colossal amount of passenger traffic. Before the mills were built the people of the Sett valley would spin and weave cloth in their own homes for their own use and to sell to increase their income. Slowly the water-powered mills overtook the cottage industry and it gradually petered out.

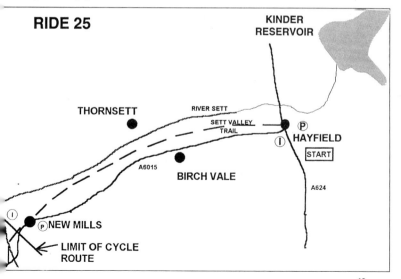

As use for the railway declined it was eventually closed in 1970 and purchased by the Derbyshire County Council in 1973.

Acknowledgement: Peak National Park Authority, Derbyshire CC, Department of Environment

The Route
Cyclists are allowed to ride the Sett Valley Trail from Hayfield to New Mills which is only 2^1/$_2$ miles long. Perhaps a little short for our use but I feel it is worthy of inclusion from the historical point of view as the trail passes through the remains of the textile industry in this area and could be linked to local roads if exploring the district by cycle.

RIDE 26: THE LADYBOWER, DERWENT & HOWDEN RESERVOIRS

Fact File
Distance: 6 to 20 miles (10 to 32km)

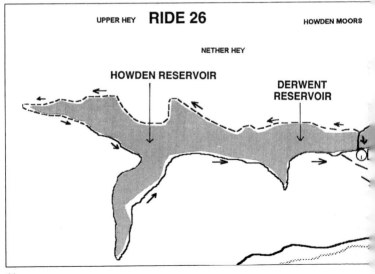

Grading: Easy on reservoir roads, moderate + on bridleways

Off Road: Up to 75% (see text)

Start: Choice of car parks around the reservoirs which soon become full. I suggest the one at OS Landranger 110 & Outdoor Leisure 1/173893 where there is a National Park information centre, cycle hire and possibly an ice cream van!

Refreshments: Do it yourself on this run!

Along the Way: Strictly scenery around the reservoirs. If the water level is low you might be able to detect the remains of Derwent village which was lost as the valley was flooded.

Acknowledgement: Severn Trent Water Authority

The Route

The Ladybower, Derwent and Howden reservoirs can be combined into one long ride of around 20 miles, or if shortcuts are taken routes of 6 miles upwards are available. There is a choice of bridleways thus increasing the off road sections if you are feeling adventurous!

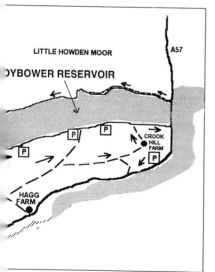

LITTLE HOWDEN MOOR

A57

YBOWER RESERVOIR

P

P

P

CROOK HILL FARM

P

HAGG FARM

If starting from the suggested car park at the side of the reservoir you have a choice of routes. You can take the circular route around Ladybower by heading off south, keeping the reservoir on your left. At the road turn left and cross the Ashopton Viaduct then take the track on the left on the other side of the reservoir towards Derwent Hamlet. The road ahead north is closed to traffic on Sundays and Bank Holidays making it an enjoyable cycle route. Watch out for locals, though, as they have a permanent right of

The fountain at Chatsworth House

way!

At the head of the Ladybower Reservoir you can follow the road round to the left and return to the start if you wish; this is a 6 mile ride. Alternatively continue north on the bridleway to cross left at the top of the Howden Reservoir to take the bridleway along the opposite side. This track eventually becomes a road, closed on Sundays and Bank Holidays, and will take you back to the car park. Alternatively you can explore the bridleways which start half way along the Derwent Reservoir. You can ride across to Hagg Farm and return via the A57, turning left just before Ashopton Viaduct to return to the car park. Or you can navigate over Bridge End Pasture and return to the reservoir via Hagg Side or ride a little further along to Crookhill Farm and return to the start area that way. Most of these bridleways are well marked with blue arrows, some having signposts as well. I will leave it to you to choose your eventual route. The bridleways are more strenuous and demand a certain amount of mountain bike riding skills. Whichever route you choose I am sure that you will enjoy the fantastic views over the reservoirs and from the bridleways across to Kinder Scout and Edale.

RIDE 27: CARSINGTON WATER

Fact File

Distance: 8½ miles (14km)

Grading: Easy

Off Road: 55%

Start: Carsington Water Visitor Centre off the B5035 between Ashbourne and Wirksworth. You can follow the signs from Ashbourne to Belper road (A517) at Hulland Ward. Alternatively all the surrounding roads are well signed to Carsington Water.

Refreshments: Carsington Water Visitor Centre

History: Carsington Water is a recently formed reservoir which belongs to Severn Trent Water. It is open for water sports, cycling, walking and horse riding.

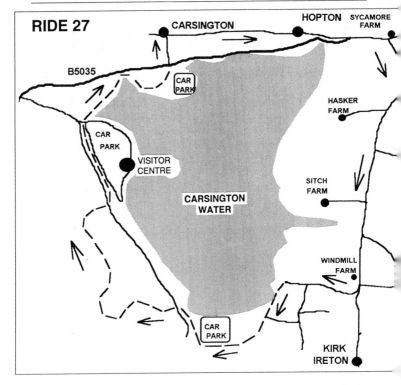

The car parks are open all the year round from 7am until dusk; a small charge is levied. There is an exhibition, shops, and a restaurant. Canoes, sailboards and cycles are available for hire.

Acknowledgement: Severn Trent Water

The Route

The suggested start is at the car park at the Visitor Centre where there are refreshment facilities. Alternatively either of the other two car parks is suitable as the route passes close by and can be picked up easily. If you prefer not to use the road section simply turn round at Carsington and retrace the route by the reservoir. The road section goes through the villages of Carsington and Hopton. On

68

leaving the latter look out for Sycamore Farm and turn right opposite onto the Kirk Ireton road. After a couple of miles, at the crossroads at Windmill Farm, turn right and rejoin the off road route round the reservoir.

RIDE 28: THE SHIPLEY COUNTRY PARK

The Shipley Country Park on the edge of the Peak District offers four routes for cyclists within its 600 acres of woodland, lakes and grassland. Shipley, once a medieval estate, was busy in the 18th century with farming and coal mining. The site was reclaimed and restoration carried out to form cycle tracks and walkways. There are some old reservoirs and plenty of parkland to explore, making Shipley Park a pleasure for the visitor to cycle around. Full recreational facilities are available here and leaflets are available from the visitor centre showing the facilities and the routes to follow. There are four routes marked on the map giving a total of more than 12 miles of different track to ride. The main car park is signed from the A608 Heanor - Derby road and the A6007 Heanor - Ilkeston road.

RIDE 29: CITY OF DERBY
CITY CENTRE TO MELBOURNE

Fact File

Distance:	8 miles (13km)
Grading:	Easy
Off Road:	100%
Start Grid Ref:	Derby. OS Landranger 128/361361
History:	The track uses part of the disused Derby Canal

and the disused Melbourne Railway.

The Route

This off road cycle track starts in the city of Derby and pleasantly

69

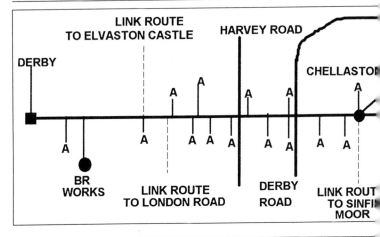

DERBY

**LINK ROUTE
TO ELVASTON CASTLE**

HARVEY ROAD

CHELLASTON

A A A A A A A

A A A A A A A A A

**BR
WORKS**

**LINK ROUTE
TO LONDON ROAD**

**DERBY
ROAD**

**LINK ROUTE
TO SINFIN
MOOR**

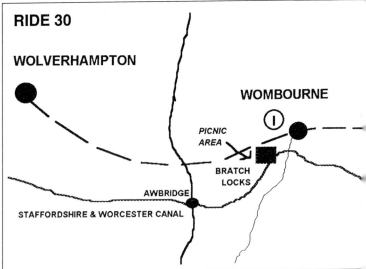

RIDE 30

WOLVERHAMPTON

WOMBOURNE

*PICNIC
AREA*

**BRATCH
LOCKS**

AWBRIDGE

STAFFORDSHIRE & WORCESTER CANAL

wends its way along to Melbourne using the old canal path and the
old Melbourne Railway. There are three short diversions - one to
Elvaston Castle alongside the river veers off to the left not far from

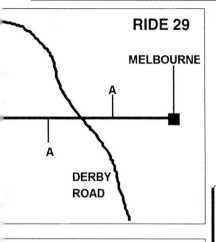

RIDE 29

MELBOURNE

A

A

DERBY ROAD

HIMLEY HALL

HIMLEY

HIMLEY HALT

KINGSWINFORD BRANCH RAILWAY PATH

PICNIC AREA

SWINDON

the start; there is a link to London Road to the right shortly after; and a few miles further along, at Chellaston, you can turn right to Sinfin Moor Lane. All three routes can be easily ridden, making a total distance of around 15 miles.

STAFFORDSHIRE

RIDE 30: KINGSWINFORD BRANCH RAILWAY TRACK

Fact File

Distance: 5¹/₂ miles (9km)

Grading: Easy

Off Road: 100%

Start Grid Ref: Wolverhampton. OS Landranger 139/877977

Refreshments: None

Along the Way: Wombourne Station, which has been restored, with picnic area and toilets, and Staffordshire & Worcestershire Canal Locks at The Bratch and Awbridge. If you do investigate these interesting areas please bear in mind that the canal path is not a right of way and a permit is required to ride.

History: The Kingswinford Branch Railway was built by

71

the Great Western Railway Company between 1912 and 1925. It closed in 1966 and was bought by the Seisdon RDC for recreational use.

Acknowledgements: South Staffordshire Council stress that the track is for occasional use and is NOT to be used for organised cycling events or races.

The Route

There is access to the track at the outskirts of Wolverhampton at Castlecroft. The track runs south for 5$^1/_2$ miles and there are many picnic areas to enjoy. Take a look at the locks on the canal as you pass nearby and the Victorian pumping station at The Bratch. Himley Wood is open to the public and is owned by the Woodland Trust. It is adjacent to Himley Station which was built for the Earl of Dudley, a director of the Great Western Railway Company, when he visited Himley Hall. Near the bridge at Bridgenorth Road climb the steps to a viewpoint. There are satisfying views over the countryside here towards Himley village and Himley Hall.

CHAPTER 4

West & South Yorkshire

RIDE 31: KIVETON PARK

Fact File

Distance:	11 miles (17km)
Grading:	Easy
Off Road:	25%
Start Grid Ref:	Wales Comprehensive School.
	OS Landranger 111/484834
Refreshments:	Pubs on route
Acknowledgement:	Rotherham Amenities & Recreation Dept

The Route

Start from the Wales Comprehensive School at Wales then take the bridleway over the railway track to Todwick. In Todwick turn right at Goose Carr Lane onto The Pastures then right again into The Meadows. Keep on this road through the estate to meet Kiveton Lane, then turn right. Just before Kiveton Hall Farm turn left onto a bridleway track to South Anston. Pass through South Anston and look out for a bridleway near the cemetery to take you across the railway and the Chesterfield Canal. Take extreme care here when crossing for the railway is very busy. At the road go left to Thorpe Salvin leaving on the Harthill road. At the crossroads go left into Packman Lane then first right along Common Road to Harthill. Leave Harthill on Woodall Lane turning right in Woodall village along Walseker Lane. In 1 mile negotiate your way back through Wales to the Comprehensive School.

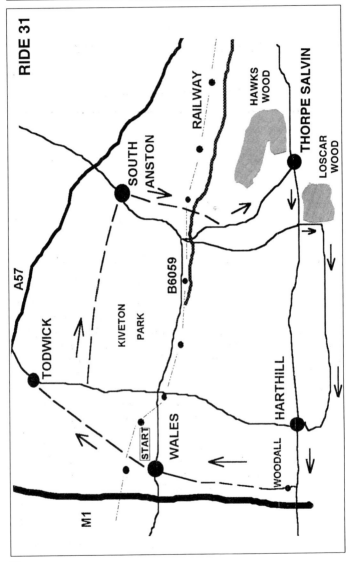

RIDE 31

RIDE 32: ULLEY COUNTRY PARK

Fact File

Distance:	9 miles (14km)
Grading:	Easy
Off Road:	15%
Start Grid Ref:	Ulley Country Park. OS Landranger 111/455876
Refreshments:	Pubs on route
Acknowledgement:	Rotherham Amenities & Recreation Dept

The Route

Starting in Ulley Country Park turn left along Reservoir Road then
right onto the A618, then shortly right along Guiltwhaite Common
Lane to Upper Whiston. Rejoin the A618, cross the bridge over the

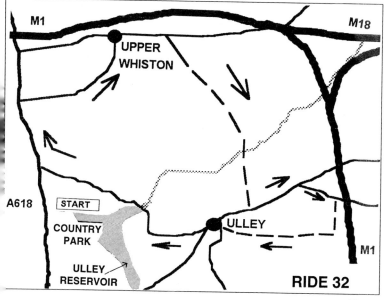

railway line then turn right along Doles Lane to touch the outskirts of Whiston. Follow this lane back over the railway and on joining a minor road at Upper Whiston go left then sharply right along Stoker Lane, a bridleway towards Ulley. At the road turn left onto Penny Hill Lane but do not go under the railway; instead turn right along High Lane that runs parallel to the railway. Follow this track that becomes Carr Lane back to Ulley where you must turn left through the village and back to the Country Park.

RIDE 33: THE WOODSETTS WOBBLE

Fact File

Distance:	13 miles (21km)
Grading:	Easy
Off Road:	40%
Start Grid Ref:	Lordens Hill Community Centre, Dinnington. OS Landranger 111/534863
Refreshments:	Pubs on route
Acknowledgement:	Rotherham Amenities & Recreation Dept

The Route

Leave the Lordens Hill Community Centre at Dinnington then turn right into Lodge Lane that leads into Red Quarry Lane. At the crossroads turn right through Gildingwells and on leaving the village look out for Home Farm on the left. Turn left adjacent to the farm along a track that leads to a bridleway in about a mile at some stone pillars.

Turn right here along the bridleway and in 1 mile turn right into Owday Lane, passing Owday Wood on the left. In a further mile turn right at the crossroads immediately past 'The Homestead' then turn left just before Cotterhill House taking the track and bridleway alongside Lindrick Golf Course. On nearing the main road, the A57(T), turn right then take the left fork along Rackford Lane. To navigate your way through Anston take the second road, Yew Tree Avenue, into the estate on the right. At the end go left along Narrow

Lane then right into Woodall Avenue and right again along Woodland Drive. Go left into Windmill Road then second right along Whitegate to Woodsetts Road where you must take the bridleway opposite. Pass Swinston Hill Wood then at Swinston Hill Road turn left towards Dinnington. In half a mile go right into High Nook Road then right again along Central Avenue. At the junction with Lordens Hill turn right and back to the Community Centre.

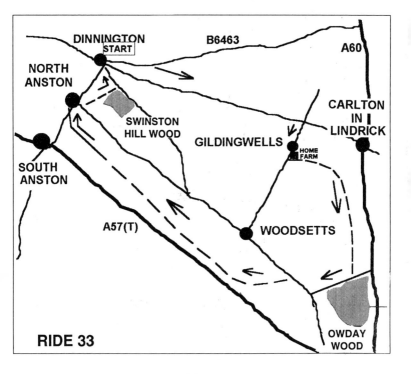

RIDE 34: THE RAVENFIELD ROMP

Fact File

Distance:	25 miles (40km)
Grading:	Easy
Off Road:	25%
Start Grid Ref:	Thryberg Country Park. OS Landranger 111/473960
Refreshments:	Pubs on route

Along the Way: Roche Abbey, 1¹/₂ miles south east of Maltby is worth a visit. This 12th-century Cistercian foundation is set in a thickly wooded valley and is surrounded by lawns. In Maltby, St Bartholmew's Church has masonry even older than Roche Abbey and has a fine stained glass window. Another church worthy of a visit is the one at Hooton Roberts; it stands on a hill overlooking the

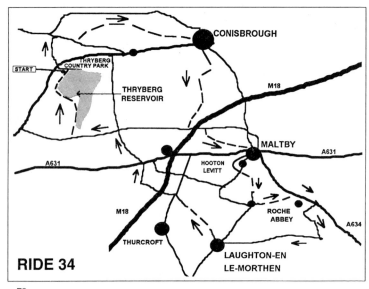

Look out for the wildfowl on the Country Park reservoirs

River Don. A visit to Conisbrough is worthy because of its 12th-century castle which has a cylindrical keep 90ft high.

History: Roche Abbey was founded in 1147 and is built over water; some buildings span the stream. It was dissolved under Henry VIII and sacked of its stone.

Acknowledgement: Rotherham Amenities & Recreation Dept

The Route
Thryberg Country Park with its lake is the starting point for this ride where there are good parking facilities. Leave the park crossing the A630 to join Carr Lane almost opposite. At the junction with the B6090 turn right then in about half a mile turn left along Howdike Lane which becomes a bridleway further along. When it meets Denaby Lane go right into Old Denaby. On leaving Old Denaby look out for Hill Top Road on the right that takes you into Conisbrough. At Old Road turn right then left into Maple Grove. Take the fourth right into Micklebring Grove which brings you to the junction with the A630. Go straight across to enter Park Lane opposite.

In 3 miles at the crossroads turn right to cross the M18, then in $^{1}/_{2}$ mile go right along Fordoles Head Lane which becomes Lilly Hall Road into Maltby. Turn into Cliff Hill on the right and at the junction with the A631 turn left, then first right into Carr Lane. Take the road into Hooton Levitt then High Hooton Road down to Slade Hooton. Follow the road round to the left to cross the railway along Gypsy Lane to the junction with the A634. Turn right here then left at Stone following the edge of King's Wood, keeping left at the end towards Firbeck. At the junction turn right then at Thwaite House look for the bridleway to the right to take you to Laughton-en-le-Morthen. On entering Laughton along St John Road turn left into Firbeck Lane and High Street. At the church the road goes right then left where you should watch out for Brookhouse Lane on the right where there are sharp bends to negotiate. Take care! At Brookhouse go straight ahead then onto a bridleway. Go straight on at the next junctions to enter Wickersley/Bramley. At the junction with the B6093 go left to Ravenfield. After crossing the old railway go left and return to Thryberg Country Park.

RIDE 35: THE FIRBECK FROLIC

Fact File

Distance:	11 miles (18km)
Grading:	Easy
Off Road:	45%
Start Grid Ref:	Lordens Hill Community Centre, Dinnington. OS Landranger 111/534863
Refreshments:	Pubs on route

Along the Way: A slight detour could be made to visit Roche Abbey which is $1^{1}/_{2}$ miles south east of Maltby. It is a 12th-century Cistercian monastery set in a thickly wooded valley.

Acknowledgement: Rotherham Amenities & Recreation Dept

The Route

Leave the Community Centre and cross into Leys Lane. Go straight

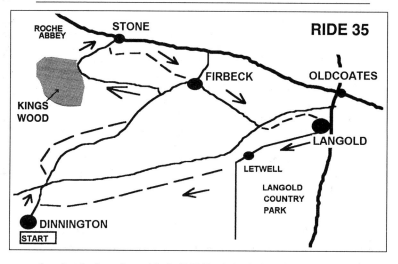

ahead at the junction with the B6463 to join the bridleway to the road at Thwaite House Farm. Take the road towards Firbeck but in ½ mile turn left along King's Wood Lane.

On entering Stone village turn sharp right onto a grassy track that becomes a bridleway, not through the farmyard. Make sure you keep to the bridleway to arrive at Firbeck on New Road. Turn left along New Road to the Black Lion Inn where the road goes sharp left. Take the bridleway along Salt Hill to the right. At the B6343 cross over to Salt Hill Road, keeping on the bridleway. At the junction turn right to Letwell. An alternative here is to go left and explore Langold Country Park and Lake then retrace your route to this point.

Leave Letwell past the church along Church Lane to meet up with another bridleway to take you back to the Community Centre at Dinnington.

CHAPTER 5
North Humberside

Additional information and historical fact about the railway routes in this chapter is available as an excellent set of route cards from shops and information services in Humberside. If difficulty is encountered please write to Humberside CC, Technical Services Dept, Countryside Section, County Hall, Beverley HU7 9XA. Or telephone during office hours 01482 867131. Acknowledgement for the tracks is appropriate to Humberside CC and the Countryside Commission.

RIDE 36: THE HULL TO HORNSEA RAILWAY LINE

Fact File

Distance: 22 or 26 miles (35 or 42km) (see text)

Off Road: 100% or 45% (see text)

Start Grid Ref: Hull, Spyvee Street. OS Landranger 107/110312

Refreshments: There are many pubs adjacent to the track as it passes close to the villages on route.

Along the Way: The track is a haven of wildlife as the old track, left to grow wild for 20 years, has formed its own wildlife habitat with the Common Spotted Orchid and Biting Stonecrop to be seen by the sharp eyed.

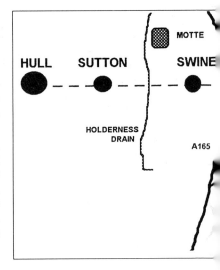

Hornsea Mere is worth a visit for its wildfowl. On the return journey visit Burton Constable Hall. It is a fine 16th-century Elizabethan house situated near the Holderness coast. Building commenced around 1570 on the site of a medieval tower house. The house today is largely a product of remodelling in the 18th century. The grounds were designed and landscaped by Capability Brown and are in a state of restoration using his original plans.

History: The Hull and Hornsea Railway Company was formed and built the railway line which was opened in 1864. Its main function was to carry tourists to Hornsea but it also carried agricultural products, animals and coal. The line was closed for economic reasons in 1964.

The Route

The railway track to Hornsea is 11 miles long and the return route to Hull can either be on the track, making a 22 mile off road route, or you may return to Hull on quiet minor roads via Burton Constable to enable a visit to this fine house to be made. If this route is chosen it would be an extra 4 miles making a round trip of 26 miles.

Starting from Spyvee Street off Cleveland Street in Hull take to

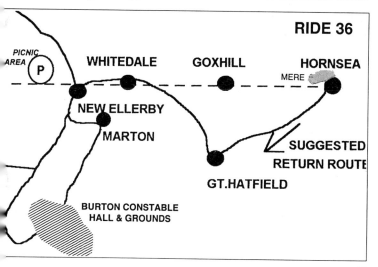

the track which goes behind the Reckitt & Colmans factory. This part of the ride is actually on the filled in Fordyke Stream, an old drainage ditch. In 1¹/₂ miles leave the stream path and join the railway track passing through Sutton on Hull.

A little further along you cross the Holderness Drain by a new bridge; just past the bridge on the left are the earthworks of an old motte and bailey castle. Soon the track arrives at Swine which has connections with the Romans and a Cistercian priory. The priory was founded in 1154 and housed both nuns and monks. Continue along past the site of Skirlaugh Station then past Dowthorpe Hall which boasts Norman fishponds in its grounds. Ellerby Station is perhaps a good place to rest and sample the fare in the nearby Railway Inn which has some railway memorabilia on display. On through Whitedale Station to Sigglesthorne Station. The village of Great Hatfield nearby has an excellent medieval cross and some fine carvings. North of the station the ground is waterlogged and a haven for marsh plants which are being studied by botanists. Please use the alternative path to conserve this important nature area. Progress onwards toward Wassend Station at Goxhill, the village named after Gauk, a Viking chief. Visit the interesting church there if you have time. From here you will see the water tower which signals that you are nearing the end of your journey in Hornsea, which has connections with the Danes; there was a settlement nearby at the deserted village of Southorpe. Be sure to visit Hornsea Mere for within its superb setting there are many different varieties of waterfowl to be seen.

When you have had your fill of seaside and mere it is time to think about the return journey. I would suggest going by road and calling to see Burton Constable Hall, a magnificent 16th-century house with over twenty rooms open to the public. Take the road to Great Hatfield out of Hornsea; if you did not visit this village on your way up from Hull now is the time to do so. Continue south west out of Great Hatfield to New Ellerby turning east here to Marton and Burton Constable. After enjoying the Hall and Grounds, and perhaps a refreshing cup of tea, make your way back to New Ellerby, join the railway track and return to Hull and your starting point.

RIDE 37: MARKET WEIGHTON TO BEVERLEY RAILWAY TRACK - Known as 'The Hudson Way'

Fact File

Distance: 11miles (16¹/₂km) one way. 22 miles (33km) return. If returning by minor roads and villages the distance would be approximately 27 miles (42km) for your return journey.

Grading: Easy

Off Road: 100% unless returning on minor roads

Start Grid Ref: Market Weighton. OS Landranger 106/882423. Map 107 required also for Beverley area.

Refreshments: Apart from the obvious facilities at Market Weighton and Beverley there is an interesting pub at Goodmanham. There are also pubs at Cherry Burton and Etton. At Kiplingcotes Station there is an antique shop called 'Grannies Attick'. Tea is available also.

Along the Way: There are many interesting features to see along the trail, including a fine selection of bridges with unusual designs. There is a quarry nature reserve between Spring Wells and Kiplingcotes Station. In fact the section between Market Weighton and Spring Wells is a nature reserve in its own right. Beverley Minster dates back to the first Saxon church around AD700.

The Minster was completed around AD1400 with restoration being carried out several times throughout the Minster's life, the most recent being between 1975 and 1986. You must visit this magnificent building.

History: The line from Market Weighton to Beverley was constructed between 1862 and 1865 with two stations: one at Kiplingcotes, the other at Cherry Burton. The line, although still profitable, was closed in 1965. Although the idea for the line came from George Hudson, who built many railway tracks in these parts, he wasn't responsible for the Market Weighton - Beverley section. However, the route is called 'The Hudson Way' in his memory.

The Route

From the centre of Market Weighton head south east and find the sign directing you to The Hudson Way along Finkle Street. Look out for Springdale Road on the left which will take you to the start of the track.

After a short stretch the track crosses a minor road then heads along Goodmanham Dale passing Spring Wells. As the name suggests there are numerous springs in the area which help to supply water for Market Weighton. The route then winds its way to Beverley. Don't forget to have a browse round Grannies Attick at Kiplingcotes Station which is a good place for a rest and some refreshment.

Spend some time in the town of Beverley with its magnificent Minster dominating the skyline. Other interesting buildings are St Mary's Church, the North Bar, Market Cross and the Guildhall.

If you wish to use an alternative route for your return why not visit the pretty villages of Bishop Burton, Cherry Burton, Etton and South Dalton, then take the minor road to Goodmanham and Market Weighton. It would add about 5 miles to your return journey.

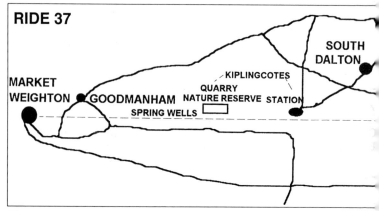

RIDE 38: THE SLEDMERE-GARTON BOTTOM WOLDS CIRCULAR

Fact File

Distance:	20 miles (32km)
Grading:	Moderate
Off Road:	38%
Start Grid Ref:	Sledmere parking area at the junction of the B1251 and the B1253. OS Landranger 101/928646
Refreshments:	The Triton Inn, Sledmere

Along the Way: Sir Tatton Sykes' monument stands erect on the Wolds. It commemorates Sir Tatton, one of the Sykes family who lived in the magnificent Sledmere House which you will catch glimpses of as you cycle around Sledmere. This Georgian house was built in 1751 and the gardens and park were designed by Capability Brown.

Note the village houses with their ornate chimneys and neat brickwork. There are many monuments worth visiting in Sledmere. Make sure you have time to see them all.

History: The wide grass road is an old Roman road, Woldgate, which connected Bridlington with York. The two villages marked on the map, Cowlam and Cottam, are deserted medieval sites. As you reach the high point of the ride on the bridleway you will notice the remains of concrete runways and old buildings. The area was a second world war airfield.

The Route

Start from the car parking area at the west end of

Sledmere at the junction of the B1251 and the B1253. Turn right out of the park and head along the B1251 for 2½ miles to a roundabout. Turn left here then in just over 1 mile turn left at the public bridleway sign along a wide grassy track, the old Roman road. Shortly cross a minor road, still following the bridleway sign. A rough grassy climb now for 2 miles to another road. You will see on the horizon Sir Tatton Sykes' monument which is at the end of the track. Cross straight over the road here, taking the minor road in front of you. In less than a mile the road bends to the left to Sledmere Grange. Leave the road here, keeping straight ahead onto a wide earth track. An exciting if bumpy downhill section takes you to Garton Bottom. At the road take the bridleway straight ahead up the grassy slope and through the gate. It is a lung bursting climb now but it soon levels off to a more gentle upward slope. Keep following the blue bridleway arrows to the top of the wold and join an old concrete airfield road. The deserted medieval village of Cottam is across the fields on your left. At the junction of bridleways keep straight on and downhill (at last) to eventually arrive at the B249. Take care on this busy road as you turn right towards Driffield. In 1 mile turn right at the sign for Cottam Warren Farm. At the farm complex follow the road round to the left and downhill to a 'T' junction in a further mile. Turn right here and enjoy the ride along

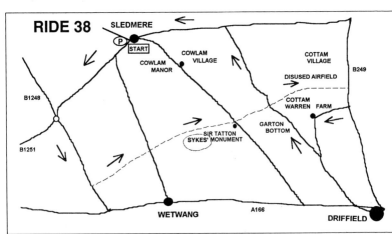

the dale of Garton Bottom and past the deserted medieval village of Cowlam. It is quite a pull along the dale for 4 miles. At the 'T' junction turn left, then right at the next 'T', to return to the car park at the other end of Sledmere village.

Part of the Hull to Hornsea railway track at Ellerby (Ride 36)

RIDE 39: THE HULL TO KEYINGHAM RAILWAY TRACK

Fact File

Distance:	8 miles (13km). 16 miles (26km) return
Grading:	Easy
Off Road:	100%
Start Grid Ref:	Southcoates Lane, Hull. OS Landranger 107/123297
Refreshments:	Pubs in Hedon and Keyingham

Along the Way: Hedon is worth a look, as is the old church at Keyingham. It contains a medieval mass dial and a 13th-century font. The construction of the church uses some unusual materials. I will let you find them for yourself.

The Route

Start at Southcoates Lane in Hull and join the track to head east towards Hedon. There is very little of scenic value along this part of

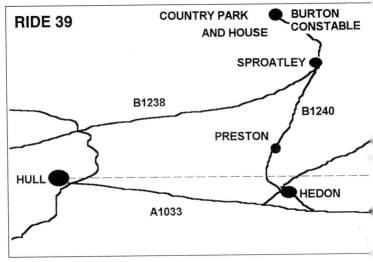

RIDE 39

COUNTRY PARK
AND HOUSE

BURTON
CONSTABLE

SPROATLEY

B1238

B1240

PRESTON

HULL

HEDON

A1033

the track; let me say it is different to all the other tracks in the book. Historic Hedon is worth looking at, an ancient market town with a square towered church called the 'King of Holderness'. Out of interest the 'Queen of Holderness' is the church at Patrington, nearer the coast.

There are water filled gravel pits on the approach to Keyingham which are used for water sports. At journey's end, Keyingham, it would be a good idea to go by road to Burton Constable via Burstwick, Elstronwick and Humbleton Manor.

A visit to the superb house there would be appropriate. You could then join up with the Hull to Hornsea railway track as described earlier in this chapter and return to Hull that way. The total distance would be approaching 30 miles (47km) for the round trip.

RIDE 40: MILLINGTON DALE AND WARTER

Fact File

Distance: 17 miles (27km)

Grading: Moderate

Off Road: 60%

Start Grid Ref: Car park at Millington Wood. OS Landranger 106/838530

Refreshments: The Gate Inn pub and the Ramblers Rest Tea Rooms in Millington village, the Wolds Inn at Huggate

Along the Way: Millington Wood is a nature reserve where the spotted woodpecker lives. Its exsistence was recorded in the Domesday Book in AD686. Visit Warter, the site of an Augustine priory near the church which was founded in 1132. Nearby was said to have been a Roman station called Delgovitia. Warter Hall, now called Warter Priory is a large modern mansion set in wooded parkland. At Huggate there is one of the

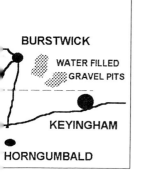

BURSTWICK

WATER FILLED
GRAVEL PITS

KEYINGHAM

HORNGUMBALD

91

deepest wells in the country; it is 298ft to the bottom.

History: Millington village is built on a Roman settlement. Many Roman remains have been found in the area with defence earthworks to be seen.

Lots of Roman remains have been found including evidence of a villa and a tessellated pavement. The church at Millington is said to be dedicated to St Margaret of Scotland and stands in a commanding position with fine views over the Wolds.

The Route
Start at the small car park at Millington Wood and turn left along Millington Dale. In just over 1 mile look out for the bridleway on the left which climbs towards a plantation. At the road turn right, then in 1 mile turn right again onto the Wolds Way. At the road junction take the left fork, pass a farm, then turn left onto the Minster Way

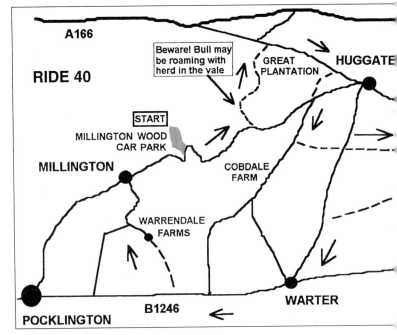

bridleway. Continue straight ahead at the road onto another bridleway. At the next road turn right then right again at the bridleway to Blanch Farm. Keep on the bridleway all the way to the road which leads to Warter. Leave Warter on the road towards Pocklington then in 2 miles turn right onto the Wolds Way bridleway through Warren Farm to Millington and along Millington Dale to the parking area.

RIDE 41: THE BUBWITH TO MARKET WEIGHTON RAILWAY PATH

Fact File

Distance:	13 miles (27km)
Grading:	Easy, but busy road at Market Weighton end
Off Road:	85%
Start Grid Ref:	Bubwith. OS Landranger 106/713358

Refreshments: If you make the journey all the way to Market Weighton ample refreshment facilities are available.

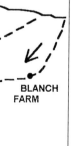

BLANCH
FARM

The Route

Turn off the A163 in Bubwith along the road signed to Breighton and Wressle. Shortly turn left along the railway track signed as a bridleway to your left. Follow the track which is signed all the way as a bridleway. The route crosses a busy road occasionally; please take care. It ends abruptly at the A163. This is a fast road so please be careful! Turn right onto the road then in a few hundred yards turn left at the roundabout onto a quieter road which leads to Market Weighton. There is no good alternative for your return journey so you must retrace your steps to proceed back to Bubwith.

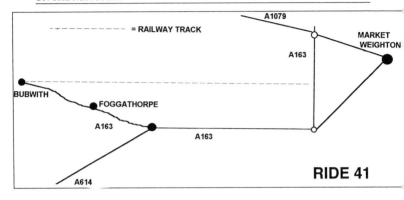

RIDE 41

The bridleway from Walesby

CHAPTER 6

Nottinghamshire

Grateful thanks must be given to Nottinghamshire County Council for the use of the following routes. Leaflets are available for additional routes both on and off road from the Rights of Way Section, Dept of P & OD, Nottinghamshire CC, Trent Bridge House, Fox Road, West Bridgeford, Nottingham NG2 6BJ. Tel:- 0115 9774483.

Also available from information centres, libraries, etc. A small charge is payable.

RIDE 42: THE DUKERIES CYCLE TRAIL
CLUMBER - SHERWOOD - THORESBY

Fact File

Distance: 22 miles (35km)

Grading: Easy

Off Road: 60%

Start Grid Ref: Clumber Park. OS Landranger 120/625745

Refreshments: Clumber Park cafe, Clumber Park Hotel, pubs and cafes at Edwinstowe, Sherwood Forest Visitor Centre, cafe

Along the Way: The Kitchen Garden Exhibition in Clumber Park. Hardwick 19th-century estate village. Clumber Lake and wildfowl. Bothamsall village, castle and church. King's Ford Bridge, ancient bridge on bridleway north of Walesby. Thoresby Hall and Lake. Budby estate village

History: The area is part of Sherwood Forest which was roamed by that loveable rogue Robin Hood. History or fable, I won't expand on the many tales that abound of this famous, or infamous character! The Dukeries were created in the 18th century when five dukes were given permission by the crown to build magnificent country estates on the land. Two superb examples remain: Welbeck Abbey, originally a monastery, and Thoresby Hall which belonged to the Dukes of Kingston.

Acknowledgement: Nottinghamshire CC

The Route
Start from the Cycle Hire Centre in Clumber Park, turning right then left past the cricket ground, riding around the perimeter and turning right onto the estate road. Go right again at signs for Hardwick village, passing Clumber Lake. Keep on the estate road through the village, cross the River Poulter then follow the Robin Hood Way signs to the A614 at the Clumber Park Hotel. Take care, great care, turning right onto the A614 and in a few yards turn off left signposted to Bothamsall. At the 'T' junction turn left and continue through the village to meet the B6387. Turn right here towards Ollerton. If you would like to try a homemade ice cream go left instead and in 1 mile call at Haughton Park Farm. Returning to the route, keep on the B6387 towards Walesby then turn right into Brake Road at the Carpenter's Arms. In approximately 1 mile after the double bend turn right onto the public bridleway, eventually joining the Robin Hood Way and crossing a footbridge over the Rivers Maun and Meden.

The Robin Hood Way takes you to the Bothamsall road. Go left here eventually meeting the A614 again. Cross with care, and take the road through Thoresby Park; the Hall and lake are to the left. Half a mile past the Lodge at the end of the estate turn left along a minor road. In front of you is Castle Budby, an 18th-century folly. At the A616 turn left into Budby village. In about $1/2$ mile turn right onto the bridleway along the edge of Budby South Forest. (The MOD warning signs do not apply to the bridleway.) In about 1 mile continue straight ahead through the plantations then in $1/2$ mile go right along the forest track bridleway, eventually meeting the road. Turn right, then at the A616, where even greater care is needed at this busy junction, join the B6034 which takes you north. At Duncan Wood Lodge turn right onto a bridleway, Freeboard Lane, which takes you to meet the A614 in about 3 miles. Turn left here then left again into Clumber Park at Drayton Gate. Follow the estate road over the bridge and back to the start area.

The Hull to Hornsea railway line
Riding the Dove Valley Trail

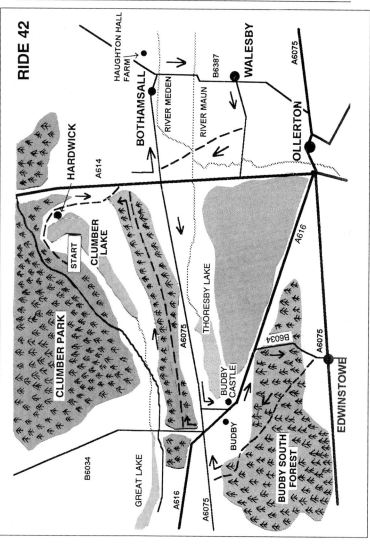

RIDE 42

HAUGHTON HALL FARM

BOTHAMSALL

HARDWICK

A614

CLUMBER LAKE

START

CLUMBER PARK

GREAT LAKE

B6034

A616

A6075

BUDBY

BUDBY CASTLE

THORESBY LAKE

RIVER MEDEN

RIVER MAUN

B6387

WALESBY

A6075

OLLERTON

A616

B6034

A6075

BUDBY SOUTH FOREST

EDWINSTOWE

Boot in Eskdale, Cumbria

RIDE 43: SHERWOOD FOREST AND THE MAUN VALLEY
MANSFIELD - SHERWOOD - EDWINSTOWE

Fact File

Distance: 15 miles (24km)

Grading: Easy

Off Road: 70%

Start Grid Ref: Mansfield. OS Landranger 120/561620

Refreshments: Sherwood Forest Visitor Centre. Edwinstowe has cafes, pubs and a restaurant.

Along the Way: The Sherwood Forest Country Park has 460 acres of woodland which was once a hunting area. Some of the forest is an SSSI (Site of Special Scientific Interest), for it is home to over 1500 species of beetle. Edwinstowe was of great importance in the middle ages in the Sherwood Forest area. You should visit St Mary's Church where it is said Robin Hood married Maid Marion. There are also the Church Farm Craft Workshops nearby if you care to have a look.

Acknowledgement: Nottinghamshire CC

The Route

Start from St Albans Church, Forest Town, Mansfield which is at the junction of Old Mill Lane, Pump Hollow Road and Clipstone Road. Free parking is available near the Prince Charles pub on Clipstone Road West about 100 yards from the church. From the church go left along Clipstone Road West taking the fourth turning left opposite the Whitegates pub into Clipstone Drive which soon turns into a track. At Cavendish Lodge take the road to the right along to the 'T' junction and turn right. At the next 'T' junction turn left signposted to Ollerton. Opposite the Dog & Duck car park turn left onto a bridleway called Archway Road. Go under the railway bridge to the junction, turn left here under the bridge then up the hill past Archway House to the road junction.

Turn right and in a few yards turn left onto the bridleway. Keep going until you arrive at a bridleway junction with the blue direction

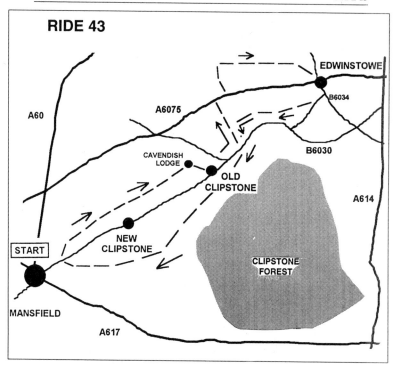

RIDE 43

EDWINSTOWE

B6034

A60

A6075

B6030

CAVENDISH LODGE

OLD CLIPSTONE

A614

NEW CLIPSTONE

START

CLIPSTONE FOREST

MANSFIELD

A617

arrows.

Turn right, keeping straight on to a junction with four tracks. Go straight on following the sign for the visitor centre where you must push your cycle and adhere to the cycling restrictions in the Country Park. There is lots to do in the Park which was part of Sherwood Forest and has changed little since the days of Robin Hood. Make your escape from the Country Park by the main exit and turn right into Edwinstowe. Visit St Mary's Church, reputed to be where Robin Hood married Maid Marion.

Keep straight on at the traffic lights and head along High Street, crossing the River Maun. In a few yards turn right along Mill Lane following signs for Mansfield and Clipstone. Shortly, at the end of the houses but before the bridge, turn right along the bridleway and re-cross the River Maun. At the junction turn left, then left again at the next junction, cross the river, under the bridge, then turn sharply to the right passing under the next bridge to meet the road at the Dog & Duck. Cross the road and pass through the Dog & Duck car park onto the bridleway passing the remains of King John's Palace on the right. The Palace was the Royal hunting centre for the Royal Forest of Sherwood. Stay on the bridleway to the junction, going straight on here through three tunnels to reach the Vicar Water Picnic Site. If you have brought your fishing tackle abandon cycling for the day, buy a day ticket, and go fishing in the lake!

Pass around the right of the water and through a tunnel. Keep straight ahead at all junctions then go through a gap by the gate, ignoring the track on the left. Continue through the farm buildings until the bridleway becomes a road near the Toray factory. At the junction go right signposted to Mansfield, Woodhouse & Worksop. Continue up the hill to the traffic lights to the start area.

Bridleways are well marked in Nottinghamshire

RIDE 44: CLUMBER PARK & CRESSWELL CRAGS

Fact File

Distance: 18 miles (30km)

Grading: Easy

Off Road: 50%

Start Grid Ref: Duncanwood Lodge Picnic Site.
OS Landranger 120/613716

Refreshments: There are pubs and cafes on the route including
The Old School House Tea Room on the B6034 near Carburton. The
Cresswell Crags Visitor Centre

Along the Way: Clumber Park and lakes, interesting old lodges
on the estate. Cresswell Crags, site of early man.

Acknowledgement: Nottinghamshire CC

The Route

Start from the Duncanwood Lodge Picnic Site at the junction with
the B6034. Cross the B6034 and ride along the bridleway, passing
Duncanwood Lodge and following the bridleway arrows to a rough
parking area at Hazel Gap. Cross the area, bearing right onto an
unsigned track. At Corunna Lodge turn right onto the road.

At the B6034 go straight ahead, taking care crossing this busy
road, and enter Clumber Park. At the crossroads turn left then
partially right following the Robin Hood Way direction sign.
Continue ahead until you meet a metalled bridleway, turn left here
and beware of traffic! At Truman's Lodge bear right then left
alongside a large gate. The track leads through the trees and
eventually to the main road. Cross with care and take the red track
opposite to Old Toll Bar Lodge. Pass the ornate Lodge along
Drinking Pit Lane, passing a pair of beautiful gates and Lady
Bolsover Drive Lodge. Soon the path forks; bear left and take a
thrilling ride downhill through sandstone cliffs. Watch out for the
right bend at the bottom of the hill then head for South Lodge. Turn
left here, passing through the deer park gates, two bridlegates and
follow the bridleway sign for Welbeck Abbey. Continue across the

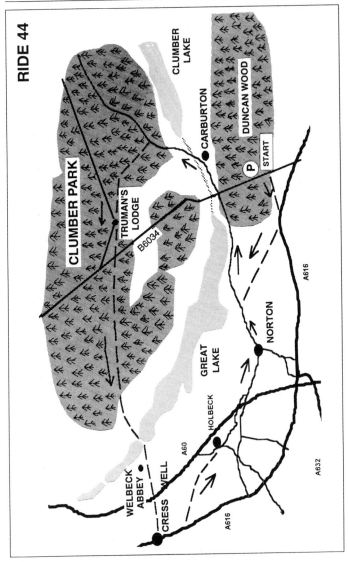

RIDE 44

CLUMBER PARK

CLUMBER LAKE

CARBURTON

DUNCAN WOOD

START

P

TRUMAN'S LODGE

B6034

GREAT LAKE

HOLBECK

NORTON

A616

A616

A632

A60

WELBECK ABBEY

CRESS WELL

track on the grass and soon you will arrive at a bridge between the waters of Gouldsmeadow Lake and Shrubbery Lake. Cross here then turn immediately right at the next junction. Shortly turn left through a bridlegate into a field and past a plantation. At the made up track turn right onto the bridleway, then follow the concrete road until you meet the A60. Go straight across here onto the bridleway opposite along a tree lined avenue, then in front of a gate turn right along a waymarked farm drive. If visiting Cresswell Crags you must walk, going through the gate before the right turn to the visitor centre. Keep on the farm path at the edge of the field until it meets the road turning left then right onto another bridleway. At the Whitwell Workshop Garage turn left towards Newark. Take care on this busy road. In less than a mile watch out for a bridleway on the left which is a walled lane to Holbeck Village. Straight on now along country lanes to Norton; take care when crossing the A60. At Norton go left at the junction signed to Carburton and Clumber. Stay on the main road until you meet some crossroads, follow the road to the right and shortly you will arrive at Corunna Lodge where you joined the route from the start. Retrace your path along this route by turning right here. Alternatively continue along to the B6034, turn right and in about a mile return to the car park at Duncanwood Lodge.

RIDE 45: THE NOTTINGHAMSHIRE FORESTS

The Forestry Commission manages six forests in the Sherwood area. Whilst they allow careful cyclists the use of forest roads in all the forests listed here there is only one waymarked cycle track. The other forests have footpaths for walkers which responsible cyclists do not ride. There are many miles of forest roads within the forest to make up your own routes. A leaflet, *The Greenwoods of Nottinghamshire*, is available from the Forestry Commission.

CLIPSTONE FOREST is the largest forest within the Sherwood complex. It contains both conifer and broadleaved trees. Fallow deer roam unhindered here but will only be seen by the sharp eyed.

There is one waymarked route for cyclists in the forest which can be accessed from the B6030 Mansfield - Ollerton road. There are two car parks and two picnic areas. The cycle route mainly follows forest roads around the perimeter of the forest and is 6 miles long.

WHITWELL WOOD is accessed from the A619 Barlborough to Worksop road and parking is in the lay-by on this road. The forest is rich in flora and has two picnic areas. There are no cycle tracks, just forest roads.

BIRKLANDS is reached from Edwinstowe and has the Sherwood Forest Visitor Centre as part of the Sherwood Country Park. No cycle tracks, roads only.

BLIDWORTH is another forest which is mainly for walkers. However the forest roads offer some good riding, with respect for the walkers of course. There are picnic areas and car parks with toilets at the northern end.

CHAPTER 7
The Yorkshire Dales

RIDE 46: PATELEY BRIDGE - GOUTHWAITE RESERVOIR - LOFTHOUSE

Fact File

Distance:　　　　　19 miles (30km)

Grading:　　　　　Moderate

Off Road:　　　　　45%

Start Grid Ref:　　　Pateley bridge. OS Landranger 99/158657

Refreshments:　　　York Arms at Ramsgill. Crown Hotel at Lofthouse. The Sportsmans Arms at Wath. Cafes and pubs in Pateley Bridge

Along the Way:　　Upper Nidderdale is surrounded by grim craggy fells rising to over 1600ft in places. There are magical names like Cockle Hill, Fountains Earth Moor and Jenny Twigs Daughter along the way. If time allows why not visit How Stean Gorge as you leave Lofthouse for the return journey? The gorge is very narrow with cliffs of 70ft on either side in places. There is a cave to explore where it is reputed a wanted criminal lived whilst avoiding arrest. There is a small charge to visit the gorge and it is signposted clearly not far from Lofthouse.

History:　　　　　The area is surrounded by ancient pot holes and caverns, some of which are open to the public. There are abandoned lead workings on the hills which are dangerous, a sign of the industrial past in the area.

The Route

Leave Pateley Bridge in a northerly direction on the Lofthouse road. Immediately across the bridge over the River Nidd turn right signposted to Wath and Lofthouse. In 1½ miles turn right over a narrow hump bridge signposted to Wath. Just past the Sportsmans

Arms go straight ahead along the bridleway which eventually takes you alongside the reservoir for 5 miles to arrive at Bouthwaite. Follow the road left here then right at the road junction at the bridge, taking the road to Lofthouse. Follow the road through Lofthouse bearing left at the entrance to Scar House Reservoir. After negotiating a sharp left bend go straight ahead leaving the main road down the track towards How Stean Gorge. In a couple of hundred yards cross the bridge and turn left at the sign for 'bridleway to Ramsgill'. If visiting the gorge turn right here before taking the route back to Ramsgill. At Ramsgill follow the road, which is part of the Nidderdale Way, alongside Gouthwaite Reservoir and back to Pateley Bridge.

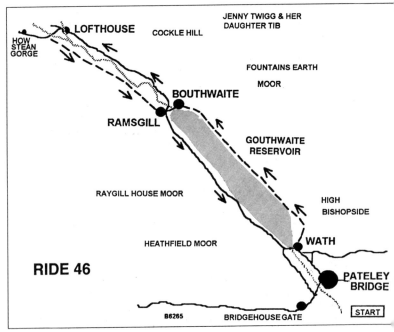

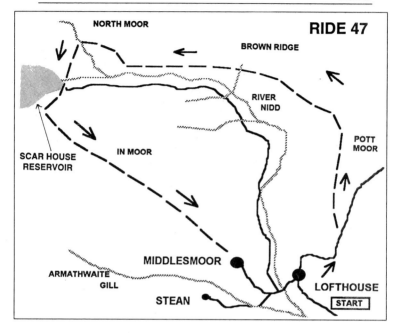

RIDE 47: LOFTHOUSE - NORTH MOOR - MIDDLESMOOR

Some navigational skills are required on this route. A map is essential and a compass would certainly be useful.

Fact File

Distance:	12 miles (19km)
Grading:	Rough & Tough
Off Road:	75%
Start Grid Ref:	Lofthouse. OS Landranger 99/101734
Refreshments:	Crown Hotel, Lofthouse
Along the Way:	The high craggy fells around this part of

107

Scar House reservoir

Nidderdale have a raw beauty of their own which contrasts with the serenity of Scar House Reservoir. Enjoy this ride but go well prepared as it is exposed over Lofthouse Moor and In Moor. Be sure to spend a little time in Middlesmoor to appreciate some of the finest views of Nidderdale from this high village. The church and churchyard are worthy of investigation for their antiquities and epitaphs.

The Route

You will need a good map on this route as some of the bridleways are undefined but they are marked on the map. Take the Masham road out of Lofthouse climbing steeply up Trapping Hill then after 1½ lung bursting uphill miles take the wide unsigned bridleway track off to the left through the gate. This is where your navigational skills come in handy! Follow this wide bridleway past Bracken Ridge, Summerstone Lodge and The Edge, then pick up a few waymarks to traverse the side of North Moor to join the Nidderdale Way down to Scar House Reservoir. Cross the dam, turn right, then in a few yards turn left following the Nidderdale Way sign onto a bridleway climbing steeply over In Moor to the village of

Middlesmoor. Take the road out of Middlesmoor for a pleasant ride back to Lofthouse.

RIDE 48: MYTHOLMROYD - HEBDEN BRIDGE - STANSFIELD MOOR - GREAT ROCK

Fact File

Distance:	17 miles (27km)
Grading:	Tough
Off Road:	30%
Start Grid Ref:	Mytholmroyd Sports Centre. OS Landranger 104 & OS Outdoor Leisure 21. GR 014260
Refreshments:	Mytholmroyd Sports Centre and various pubs and cafes at Hebden Bridge and on route

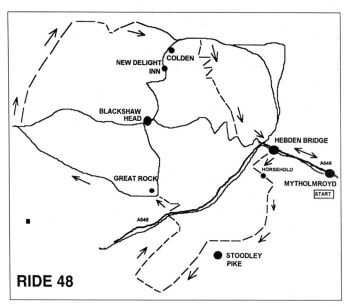

RIDE 48

Along the Way: The route crosses exposed ground with good views of Stoodley Pike and Great Rock.

Acknowledgement: Calderdale Council. Route Guides for all Calderdale Council rides are available from the tourist information centre at Hebden Bridge.

The Route

Start at the Sports Centre in Caldene Avenue at Mytholmroyd. An advantage of parking here is that there are showers and changing facilities available, albeit for a small fee. From the sports centre turn left to take the A646 Hebden Bridge road. Go straight across the lights in Hebden Bridge then turn left after the supermarket. Cross the canal and turn right taking the sign to Horsehold. A good climb now on tarmac road which turns to cobbles a little further along. At Horsehold go right onto the old packhorse road, then at the crossroads turn right towards Stoodley Pike. The views from the pike are outstanding. After passing some farms keep straight ahead and when the Pennine Way crosses your path begin to descend until the path joins a wall on the right. Follow this then turn right just before the next gate signed to Stoodley. Descend as far as the hospital then go right. The road eventually becomes a rough track; keep straight ahead and down to a stream. Turning left over the stream follow the track until it forks left downhill to a gate. Go through the gate and cross the canal. Turn left onto the A646 then shortly right under a bridge into Duke Street. Follow the road to the right and climb through the woods up the valley side. This is a tough climb which will test your aerobic qualities to the full! Pass through a farm to reach a road below Great Rock. Go to the left of Great Rock and keep on climbing for about a mile, turning right at the end of Eastwood Road then shortly left into Dukes Cut. Keep on the track then turn left through a gate signposted Colden. Downhill now, through another gate, still following the Colden signs.

At the tarmac lane by a stream go straight across at Land Bridge then uphill to Edge Lane. Keep on Edge Lane as far as Colden. At Colden turn left past a row of cottages on the right and go downhill towards Slack. Just before reaching Slack at the bottom of the hill turn right onto a path then left towards the row of cottages. Go past the cottages on the right then take the bridleway sign through a gate.

Downhill going left, right, then left fork at the edge of the wood. Downhill through the wood to a stream, cross the stream and go up the other side bearing left. Keep straight ahead now until you reach the road. Go to the left past the church to the main road, turning left and back to Mytholmroyd.

RIDE 49: HARDCASTLE CRAGS - GORPLE RESERVOIR - HEBDEN BRIDGE

Fact File

Distance:	11 miles (17$^{1/}$₂km)
Grading:	Moderate
Off Road	50%
Start Grid Ref:	Hardcastle Crags. OS Landranger 103 & OS Outdoor Leisure 21. GR 969299
Refreshments:	Cafes are plentiful in Hebden Bridge, pubs along route
Along the Way:	The Lower Gorple Reservoir, Views
Acknowledgement:	Calderdale Council

The Route

Start from the National Trust car park at Hardcastle Crags which is signposted off the A6033. Turn left out of the car park then almost immediately right past Hollin Hall. Keeping straight ahead the track climbs then levels out a little where a track climbs off to the left. Take this track past some farms and the houses at Walshaw, descending eventually to cross Alcomden Water. Pass through a gate then bear right to meet a concrete road.

Take the next fork left then left again to meet the road, turning left as far as the steel gates a little further on the right. Turn right here onto the bridleway across Yorkshire Water property. The bridleway leads up to the Lower Gorple Reservoir and crosses the dam wall. Go left at Gorple Cottages and in a few yards right over the bridge climbing up to Heptonstall Moor. Continue along this track without

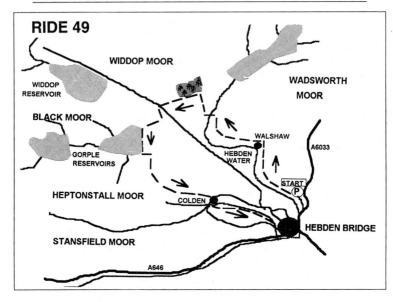

RIDE 49

WIDDOP MOOR

WIDDOP RESERVOIR

WADSWORTH MOOR

BLACK MOOR

WALSHAW

A6033

GORPLE RESERVOIRS

HEBDEN WATER

START P

HEPTONSTALL MOOR

COLDEN

HEBDEN BRIDGE

STANSFIELD MOOR

A646

deviation ignoring the right turns just after the gate. Follow Edge Lane to the road at Colden turning right here to the New Delight Inn. Seventy-five yards past the inn go left onto a bridleway to take you to Hebden Bridge. Take care here, as walkers and sometimes cars will be using the track. Join the road at the bottom by turning left, pass the church then go left onto the A646 passing through the traffic lights into Hebden Bridge. At the traffic lights in the centre of town turn left to return to Hardcastle Crags car park.

RIDE 50: LITTONDALE & LANGSTROTHDALE
BUCKDEN - RAISGILL - HALTON GILL - LITTON

Fact File

Distance: 12 miles (19km)

Grading: Rough & Tough

112

Off Road:	60%
Start Grid Ref:	Car park at Buckden. OS Outdoor Leisure 30/Landranger 98/942772

Refreshments: The Buck Inn Hotel at Buckden, The Queens Arms at Litton, The George Inn at Hubberholme

Along the Way: Solitude, views and thrilling descents are what you will remember about this route, apart from bursting lungs and aching limbs of course!

Acknowledgement: John Keavey

The Route

Be prepared on this route; take some food and extra clothing. The moors can be exposed and cruel at ANY time of year. Leave the car park at Buckden and head off in a westerly direction on the road to the picturesque village of Hubberholme with its quaint church, then continue along to Raisgill. In about 2¹/₂ miles at Raisgill follow the sign off left 'Bridleway to Halton Gill'. This is a rough, hard, sometimes undefined track over Horse Head Moor climbing to

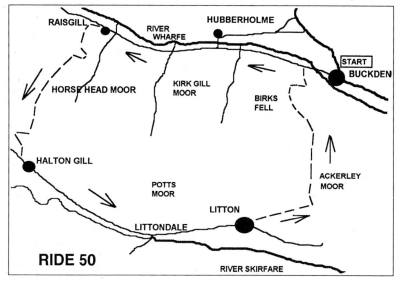

RIDE 50

almost 1900ft, but well worth the effort for the views alone. Descend into Halton Gill and turn left into the village to ride along Littondale for 2 miles into the village of Litton. Perhaps it is time to take some refreshment at the Queens Arms before tackling the next section of the route!

At the side of the Queens Arms take the bridleway signed 'BW to Buckden', and tackle your second steep climb of the day over Ackerley Moor and Birks Fell. The advantage of such a steep climb is the scintillating bash down the other side! At the road turn right and return to the car park at Buckden about half a mile away.

RIDE 51: THE ROMAN RUN
BUCKDEN - SEMERWATER - ROMAN ROAD - LANGSTROTHDALE

Fact File

Distance:	24 miles (38km)
Grading:	Rough & Tough
Off Road:	45%
Start Grid Ref:	Car park at Buckden. OS Outdoor Leisure 30/Landranger 98/942772
Refreshments:	Buck Inn at Buckden. The George Inn at Hubberholme

Along the Way: Fantastic wild scenery contrasts with the tranquil Semerwater and will perhaps make you forget the severity of this ride. The Roman road takes you in a straight line across Wether Fell to around 1800ft. The view from here over Wensleydale is breathtaking.

Acknowledgement: John Keavey

The Route

Start from the car park in Buckden and take the bridleway at the rear of the park. This is a tough climb over Buckden Rake which eventually meets the Bishopdale road in about a mile and a half. Turn right at the road and near the summit turn left at grid ref

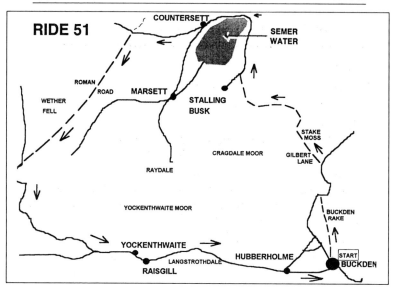

943804 onto the track called Gilbert Lane. Follow the track as it climbs over Stake Moss then on to Stalling Busk. Where the track forks previous to Stalling Busk go right along High Lane to Stake Road. Take the road north round the head of Semerwater Lake to Countersett. Leave Countersett in a westerly direction to climb up Crag Side Road towards Burtersett and Hawes. As you speed downhill at the approach to a sharp right bend watch out for the Roman road that crosses at Four Lane Ends. Turn left onto the road and climb up to Wether Fell and eventually join the Hawes road. Turn left here and shortly left again taking the Outershaw road then left again towards Buckden.Take extreme care as you cycle down this steep road as there are lots of tight hairpin bends! Hopefully having arrived safely at the bottom of Langstrothdale Chase enjoy the beautiful and peaceful Langstrothdale as you make your way to Hubberholme and on to Buckden where some well earned refreshment awaits at the Buck Inn.

RIDE 52: KETTLEWELL - STARBOTTON - ARNCLIFFE

Fact File

Distance:	6½ miles (9km)
Grading:	Rough & Tough
Off Road:	60%
Start Grid Ref:	Car park at Kettlewell. OS Outdoor Leisure 30 and 10 are required. GR 970725
Refreshments:	Pubs and cafes in Kettlewell

Along the Way: Climbing to around 1600ft at Cam Head and Old Cote Moor make the scenic quality of this ride the dominant factor. Explore Kettlewell if time allows.

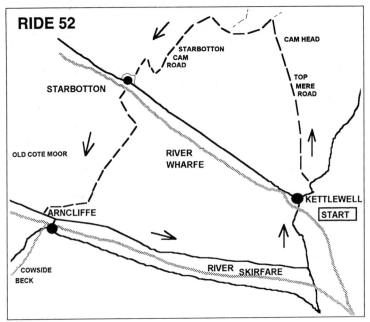

The Route
Take the very steep and narrow Leyburn road out of Kettlewell. Soon the road turns sharp left then sharp right. Instead of following the road at the right turn go straight ahead onto a wide stony track (Top Mere Road), signposted to Cam Head. Continue along to the summit then take the bridleway left past Sandy Gate and soon onto Starbotton Cam Road which takes you downhill to Starbotton village. Cross the B6160 and follow the bridleway sign to Arncliffe over the River Wharfe then across Old Cote Moor. At the road turn left following the route of the River Skirfare. When you meet the B6160 again turn left and return to Kettlewell.

CHAPTER 8
The Trans Pennine Trail

The Trans Pennine Trail is an ambitious project to build a route for cyclists, walkers and horse riders from the port of Liverpool on the west coast to the port of Hull on the east coast. There will be links to some of the great cities alongside the route and the surface which cyclists use will be hard. The project involves 30 local authorities, Raleigh Industries, the Countryside Commission and Sustrans. When finished it will be over 150 miles (240km) in length using disused railways, canal towpaths, rights of way and riverside paths. It is hoped that accommodation and other facilities will be introduced to enable the length of the trail to be traversed easily. When completed it could connect up via the King George Dock at Hull to a network of long distance routes on the continent. They extend via Holland, Germany and Czechoslovakia into Northern Turkey. Now that would be some ride!

Although the Trans Pennine Trail is only just over half complete there are several rewarding and scenic rides which can be accomplished. This chapter highlights the sections currently available, although it must be pointed out that the brief maps are for guidance only and the route should be plotted on the appropriate Ordnance Survey map, or the official leaflet for the trail consulted (available from the Trans Pennine Trail Officer, address below) before setting out on the ride. A word of warning! If you intend riding on the public roads which are open to vehicular traffic between completed sections of the Trans Pennine Trail please take extreme care!

Individual leaflets on all completed sections of the Trans Pennine Trail as well as a guide entitled 'Walking the Trail' are available from Pam Ashton, Trans Pennine Trail Officer, C/O Department of Planning, Barnsley Metropolitan Borough Council, Central Offices, Kendray Street, Barnsley S70 2TN.

Cyclists must take note that the trail is a combined user route, as are most of the routes in this book, and they should take care to give way to and be respectful to other users.

ACKNOWLEDGEMENTS

The Trans Pennine Trail would not have existed without the hard work, co-operation and grants to provide some of the finance for the trail.

Acknowledgement is therefore appropriate to the following:

The County Councils of Cheshire, Derbyshire, Humberside, North Yorkshire, and Lancashire.

The Metropolitan District Councils of Barnsley, Doncaster, Knowsley, Leeds, Liverpool, Manchester, Rotherham, Sefton, Sheffield, Stockport, Tameside, Trafford and Wakefield.

The City Councils & Shire Districts of Beverley, Boothferry, Chesterfield, Halton, High Peak, Holderness, Hull, NE Derbyshire, Selby, Warrington, West Lancashire and York.

Other Authorities: Peak Park Joint Planning Board and the Greater Manchester Countryside Unit.

The Major Sponsors are the Countryside Commission, The Department of the Environment including the City Challenge Grant, Derelict Land Grant (DLG), Neglected Land Grant (NLG) and the Urban Programme, The Merseyside Task Force (DLG and NLG), The Department of Transport, The European Union, British Rail, The National Rivers Authority, Sustrans, Raleigh and North West Water.

The developing trail will gradually be handed over to the countryside managers including many local authority Countryside Management and Ranger Services assisted by a great many voluntary rangers of different types.

Thanks are also appropriate to Pam Ashton, Trans Pennine Trail Officer, for her assistance and patience in helping me to produce this chapter on the Trans Pennine Trail.

RIDE 53: THE CHESHIRE LINES PATH
AINSDALE TO MAGHULL

Fact File

Distance:	10 miles (16km)
Grading:	Easy
Off Road:	100%
Start Grid Ref:	Plex Moss Lane. OS Landranger 108/325102
Leaflet Available:	The Sustrans Cheshire Lines Path

The Route

The Cheshire Lines Path of 10 miles inherits its name from the Cheshire Lines Railway Company. They operated services between Liverpool and Southport. Our cycle route runs from Ainsdale to Maghull. The Cheshire Lines path starts at Plex Moss Lane where there is access to the disused railway track. It can be linked with the Liverpool Loop Line by road to form a 20 mile ride. There are several access points along the route, the most southerly being at Green Lane, Maghull.

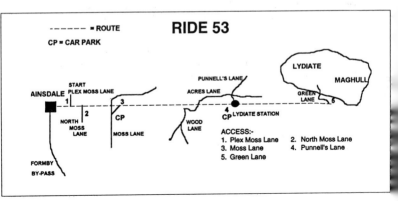

RIDE 54: THE LIVERPOOL LOOP LINE
AINTREE TO HALEWOOD

Fact File

Distance:	10 miles (16km)
Grading:	Easy
Off Road:	100%
Start Grid Ref:	Rice Lane Recreation Ground. OS Landranger 108/367961
Leaflet Available:	The Sustrans Liverpool Loop Line Railway Path

The Route

The Liverpool Loop Line is the basis of a project to create a landscaped path all the way from Halewood to Southport. The present path is open from the Rice Lane Recreation Ground to the Halewood Triangle Country Park. You can join the Liverpool Loop Line at Hartley Avenue and continue along the path to finish at the Halewood Country Park. There are many access points along the route giving an infinite choice of entry.

There are a couple of short sections further east: at Pickerings Pasture, which starts at GR 108/488838 and continues for about a mile using sections of the Mersey Way, and at the St Helens Canal in Halton and Warrington which is approximately 5 miles (8km) starting from Spike Island GR 108/514843 to GR 108/585877.

- - - - = ROUTE

RIDE 54

| RICE LANE RECREATION GROUND | FAZAKERLY | NORRIS GREEN | WEST DERBY | KNOTTY ASH | | HALEWOOD COUNTRY PARK |

○ – ○

START   BROADWAY   BOWRING PARK   GATEACRE   FINISH

CHILDWALL   WOOLTON

THERE ARE MORE THAN 20 EASILY FOUND ACCESS POINTS TO THE PATH

RIDE 55: A ROUTE THROUGH GREATER MANCHESTER

Fact File

Distance:	6 miles (10km)
Grading:	Easy
Off Road:	90%
Start Grid Ref:	Hawthorn Road. OS Landranger 109/800937
Leaflet Available:	Greater Manchester Area

The Route - Part 1

The route is still at the planning stage from the River Bollin (boundary between Warrington and Trafford) and Hawthorn Road (boundary between Trafford and Manchester). From Hawthorn Road to the Stockport end of the Midland Railway Path the route is available for cyclists but is rather rough along the River Mersey.

Start at Hawthorn Road and follow it along to the River Mersey. Keep on the north bank of the Mersey for about 5 miles (8km) and after passing Simon's Bridge turn left along Ford Lane. At the end of Ford Lane turn right then right again into Wilmslow Road (A5145). Cross at the traffic lights and turn left into Didsbury Park. Cross the park and join the Midland Railway Path at Didsbury for about a mile.

In Stockport work on the Trans Pennine Trail along the River Mersey will begin soon. Meanwhile it is only footpath status and out of bounds to cyclists.

The Route - Part 2

Fact File

Distance:	4 miles (7km)
Grading:	Easy
Off Road:	80%
Start Grid Ref:	Tiviot Dale car park. OS Landranger 109/902913
Leaflet Available:	Greater Manchester Area

Start at the car park at Tiviot Dale and follow the Railway Path and signs to the Reddish Vale Visitor Centre. Go to Mill Lane passing the millponds on the right and the visitor centre on the left. Turn right and right again through the barrier into Ross Lane which is a public bridleway. Continue over the M66 and past Hyde Hall Farm. Take the first turning to the right into Kingsley Close and wheel your cycle through the muddy footpath which connects to Chillington Walk. Cycle to and left along Yew Tree Road to Stockport Road. Please take extra care on this major road as you turn right onto it. Keep straight on for about 200 yards then take the left turning onto the Hulmes Wood bridleway.

Follow the bridleways along the River Tame through Hulmes Wood and Haughton Dale, turning right at GR 934933 along Meadow Lane to return to the River Tame again. Continue through Haughton Dale to Gibraltar Bridge. This is the end of the route at present so you could retrace your steps to return to the car park at Tiviot Dale or go left over the canal, under the railway and return on the roads. If you choose this option please take extreme care on these busy roads.

RIDE 56: WARRINGTON

There are not many local authorities who have a complete Trans Pennine Trail route from one boundary to the other but Warrington Borough Council have achieved just that, although certain improvements are in hand along the route.

The 4½ mile (7km) Railway Path from Bradshaw Lane at Latchford to Heatley is complete and should be open to walkers, cyclists and horse riders for most of the way by 1995, with all the landscaping and planting being complete.

The 1½ mile (2km) section along the north bank of the Manchester Ship Canal is also complete from London Road swing bridge to Knutsford Road.

Both these sections are extremely attractive and it is hoped that the improvements will be completed during 1995 A leaflet *95 Events* is available from Warrington Borough Council.

RIDE 57: THE LONGDENDALE TRAIL
HADFIELD TO PENISTONE

Distance:	16¹/₂ miles (26km)
Grading:	Moderate
Off Road:	75%
Start Grid Ref:	Platt Street, Hadfield. OS Landranger 110/024961
Leaflet Available:	From North West Water, The Longdendale Trail

The Route

The Longdendale Trail uses the old railway track between Hadfield and Woodhead then bridleways at Longsides and Saltersbrook and a minor road to Dunford Bridge. Join the route at Platt Street and head along the south side of Bottoms Reservoir in an easterly direction. The Longdendale Trail takes you to the A628 at Woodhead Tunnel. Cross the road with care and head eastwards along a

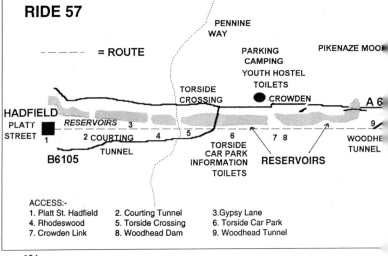

mixture of bridleways and paths crossing the A628 and joining the bridleway at Saltersbrook to join a minor road at Windle Edge, heading north east to Dunford Bridge.

The intended route for the Trans Pennine Trail will eventually use the disused Woodhead railway line from Dunford Bridge to Penistone, but until it is acquired from British Rail cyclists will have to take to the road to complete the section to Penistone. The Longdendale Trail is a most beautiful part of the Trans Pennine Trail. Along the way there is a campsite nearby, a youth hostel, information centres and several picnic areas.

RIDE 58: THE DOVE VALLEY TRAIL
SILKSTONE COMMON TO WOMBWELL

Fact File

Distance:	6 miles (9½km)
Grading:	Easy
Off Road:	100%
Start Grid Ref:	Moor End Lane, Silkston Common. OS Landranger 110/295040
Leaflet Available:	The Dove Valley Trail

History: The western part of the route uses the track of the Worsborough Bank Railway that carried coal traffic to Lancashire.

It has one of the steepest gradients in the country and a special engine, a Beyer Garrett 2-8-8-2, was designed and built to assist the 850 ton coal trains over the bank. The locomotive was the largest steam engine in Britain and could be heard working several miles away in Barnsley. The line was closed in 1981 due to the decline in coal traffic.

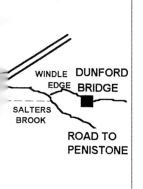

WINDLE EDGE DUNFORD BRIDGE

SALTERS BROOK

ROAD TO PENISTONE

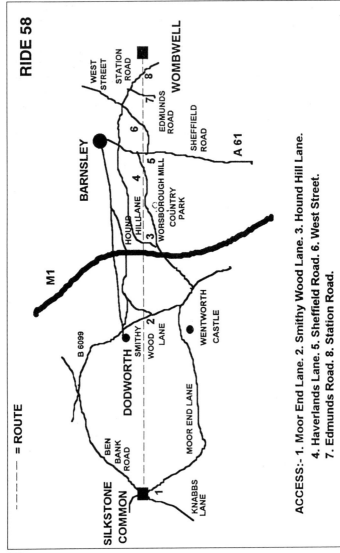

RIDE 58

ACCESS:- 1. Moor End Lane. 2. Smithy Wood Lane. 3. Hound Hill Lane.
4. Haverlands Lane. 5. Sheffield Road. 6. West Street.
7. Edmunds Road. 8. Station Road.

The Route

From the previous section leave Penistone on the B6462 as far as Oxspring then turn left to Silkstone Common which is the start of the Dove Valley Trail. This section of the Trans Pennine Trail passes through some glorious countryside as it heads east through the outskirts of Barnsley with beautiful landscape across to Wentworth Castle. Close by is the Worsborough Country Park which is a haven for wildlife, with the Mill Museum within the grounds. The Worsborough Reservoir was built to feed a canal and is the heart of the country park. In the same area is Wigfield Farm which is open to the public.

The planned route in Barnsley Borough is all on disused railways but until they are available cyclists must use road links to reach the Dove Valley Trail. The route starts at Moor End Lane, Silkstone Common and winds its way along the old railway track to finish via Aldham Junction into Station Road, Wombwell.

RIDE 59: THE AIRE - CALDER NAVIGATION TOWPATH

This link is not quite ready for use yet. Please check with the local authority before attempting to ride it.

Fact File

Distance:	$3^{1}/_{2}$ miles ($5^{1}/_{2}$km)
Grading:	Easy
Off Road:	90%
Start Grid Ref:	Leeds. OS Landranger 104/309330.

Although not usable at the time of writing the Aire - Calder Navigation Towpath will, when completed, connect users from Leeds and Wakefield onto the Trans Pennine Trail in the Barnsley area.

The start will be at GR 104/309330 and will follow the canal path to Woodlesford, GR 104/370292.

RIDE 60: THE YORK & SELBY PATH
YORK TO SELBY

Fact File

Distance: 15 miles (24km)

Grading: Easy

Off Road: 80%

Start Grid Ref: Terry Avenue, York. OS Landranger 105/604512

History: The cycle track uses the old East Coast Main Line that was closed in 1983 when a diversion was opened to by-pass the area of the Selby coalfield. Sustrans bought the track north of Riccall to provide a traffic free path for pedestrians and cyclists. It was opened in 1987.

South of Riccall the track was bought by the Department of Transport to make the Riccall to Barlby by-pass. A cycle track was made alongside the by-pass to avoid cyclists having to cross or use the A19.

Leaflet Available: York & Selby Railway Path & Cycle Route

The Route

The route starts at Terry Avenue in York and follows the River Ouse as far as the Knavesmire Racecourse. Cross the Bishopthorpe road then follow the cycle route across the racecourse. In Bishopthorpe it is necessary to cycle on a cycle track for part of the way to join the railway path as directed. At Riccall you leave the track and join a specially constructed path alongside the new A19 and then follow the old A19 into Barlby. You must leave Barlby on the Selby road and join the river bank cycle path opposite the roundabout.

If you are riding the next leg of the Trans Pennine Trail to Howden leave Barlby either on the A63, which is very busy, or preferably take to the quieter roads via Osgodby to take you to Cliffe.

Tough going in the Lake District
Wigan Pier - the start of Ride 75

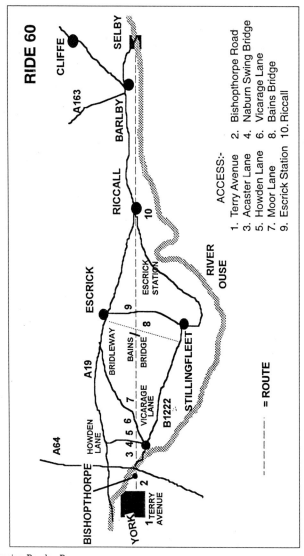

RIDE 60

ACCESS:-
1. Terry Avenue 2. Bishopthorpe Road
3. Acaster Lane 4. Naburn Swing Bridge
5. Howden Lane 6. Vicarage Lane
7. Moor Lane 8. Bains Bridge
9. Escrick Station 10. Riccall

– – – – – = ROUTE

Crossing Rowley Burn

RIDE 61: SELBY TO HOWDEN

Fact File

Distance:	10 miles (16km)
Grading:	Easy
Off Road:	30%
Start Grid Ref:	Selby. OS Landranger 105/620323
Leaflet Available:	Trans Pennine Trail Howden to Selby

The Route

The continuation of the Trans Pennine Trail cycle route from Selby now takes the road to Cliffe, (see previous section for route details). Due to a right of way dispute the portion of off road track and lane between Selby and Cliffe is out of bounds to cyclists at the moment. For the latest update on this path you should contact The Rights of Way officer for North Yorkshire on 01904 628746. Having reached Cliffe by road, head for the A63 leaving towards Hemingbrough and look out for the specially prepared cycle track alongside the A63

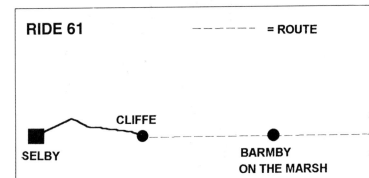

RIDE 61 — — — — — — = ROUTE

CLIFFE

SELBY

BARMBY
ON THE MARSH

THE OFF ROAD ROUTE BETWEEN SELBY AND CLIFFE
IS OUT OF BOUNDS TO CYCLISTS AT THE MOMENT.
YOU MUST USE THE ROAD.(SEE TEXT)

which goes from Cliffe to Hemingbrough. Leave Hemingbrough along Landing Lane towards the River Ouse. At the river bank cyclists must now use the specially constructed cycle path at the base of the flood bank. At the Barmby Barrage you must dismount and wheel your cycle across to join minor roads to visit Barmby on the Marsh through Asselby, Knedlington and Howden to finish at Kilpin Pike.

RIDE 62: THE HORNSEA RAIL TRAIL

Distance:	13 miles (21km)
Off Road:	100%
Start Grid Ref:	Spyvee Street, Hull. OS Landranger 107/108297

Leaflet Available: Hull Hornsea Railway Line from Humberside CC, Technical Services Dept, Countryside Section, County Hall, Beverley HU7 9XA. Tel: 01482 867131. The leaflet is in fact a set of route cards. A charge is made for this well presented and very informative publication.

Along the Way: The track is a haven of wildlife as the old track, left to grow wild for 20 years, has formed its own wildlife habitat with the Common Spotted Orchid and Biting Stonecrop to be seen by the sharp eyed. Hornsea Mere is worth a visit to see the wildfowl. Burton Constable Hall is worthy of a diversion to see the hall, a fine 16th-century Elizabethan house situated near the Holderness coast. Building commenced around 1570 on the site of a medieval tower house.

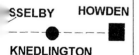

The house today is largely a product of remodelling in the 18th century. The grounds were designed and landscaped by Capability Brown and are in a state of restoration using information from his original plans.

History: The Hull and Hornsea Railway Company was formed and built the railway line which was opened in 1864. Its main function was to carry tourists to Hornsea but it also carried agricultural products, animals and coal. The line was closed for economic reasons in 1964.

The Route
Starting from Spyvee Street off Cleveland Street in Hull take to the track that goes behind the Reckitt & Colmans factory. This part of the ride is actually on the filled in Fordyke Stream, an old drainage ditch. In about ³/₄ mile leave the stream path and join the railway track passing through Sutton on Hull.

A little further along you cross the Holderness Drain by a new bridge. Just past the bridge on the left are the earthworks of an old motte and bailey castle.

Soon the track arrives at Swine which has connections with the Romans and a Cistercian priory. The priory was founded in 1154 and housed both nuns and monks. Continue along past the site of Skirlaugh Station then past Dowthorpe Hall that boasts Norman fishponds in its grounds.

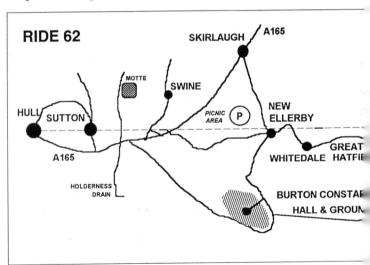

132

This water tower is visible for miles around in Humberside. When you reach the tower you are almost at journey's end at Hornsea

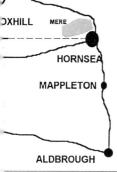

Ellerby Station is perhaps a good place to rest and sample the fare in the nearby Railway Inn that has some railway memorabilia on display. On through Whitedale Station to Sigglesthorne Station. The village of Great Hatfield nearby has an excellent medieval cross and some fine carvings. North of the station the ground is waterlogged and a haven for marsh plants which are being studied by botanists. Please use the alternative path to conserve this important nature area. Progress onwards toward Wassand Station at Goxhill, the village named after Gauk, a Viking chief, and visit the interesting church there if you have time.

From here you will see the water tower that signals that you are nearing the end of your journey in Hornsea. It has connections with the Danes; there was a settlement nearby at the deserted village of Southorpe. Be sure to visit Hornsea Mere for within its superb setting there are many different varieties of waterfowl to be seen.

CHAPTER 9
Cumbria

Cumbria offers some of the most rewarding off road riding in the north of England, although the majority of routes are extremely tough. Riding in the winter months when the fells are dressed in a coat of white snow is an unbelievable experience, but beware of the wind chill factor. Correctly attired, all season riding is available in Cumbria if you choose your routes and treat them with respect.

RIDE 63: CONISTON AND WALNA SCAR

Fact File

Distance:	17 miles (27km)
Grading:	Rough & Tough
Off Road:	30%
Start Grid Ref:	Coniston. OS Landranger 96/303976

History: The Walna Scar road is no more than a rough track connecting Coniston with Dunnerdale. It was used by packhorses and is in fact an ancient mountain pass littered with Bronze Age relics, a Bronze Age cemetery and even the odd stone circle. If you are fortunate you might see a flying saucer as a photograph of one was taken nearby.

In the 18th century during the mining and quarrying boom horse-drawn carts struggled along the road with their heavy loads of slate. Although the Walna Scar Pass is only 2000ft above sea level it must have been a difficult and dangerous crossing for the waggoners.

The Route

Leave Coniston on the Torver road and before leaving the town, near the bridge, look out for the uphill road on the right and the sign for Walna Scar. It is a hard pull up this road which soon becomes a

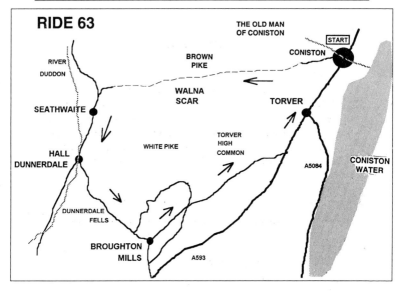

track. After 2 miles follow signs for Walna Scar. The road, or track as it is, continues under the shadow of Coniston Old Man until it eventually becomes steeper as it climbs to the summit at Walna Scar. Take care on the steep descent; brakes are likely to become hot and melt your wheel rims!

At the road in Dunnerdale head left towards Seathwaite then at Hall Dunnerdale keep left to take you over the Dunnerdale Fells to Broughton Mills. Left again here then straight on to join the main road to Torver and Coniston.

RIDE 64: THRELKELD - SKIDDAW HOUSE - MUNGRISDALE

Fact File

Distance:	16 miles (26km)
Grading:	Rough & Tough
Off Road:	40%

136

Start Grid Ref: Threlkeld village car park. OS Landranger
                    90/320254 or alternatively Bassenthwaite
                    90/231322. See text

Refreshments: At Threlkeld there is The Salutation Inn and the
Horse & Farrier. The Mill Inn at Mungrisdale

The Route

There is a choice of start and track for this ride making two good
routes using the common track from Skiddaw House to Mosedale.
The recommended start is at Threlkeld where there is a village car
park and good refreshment facilities.

The route is flanked on the right by the grandeur of Blencathra,
popularly known as Saddleback, and the magnificence of the
Skiddaw range on the left with the peak of Skiddaw prominent.
Turn right out of the Threlkeld village car park and ride along the
road following signs for the Blencathra Centre. Shortly turn right at
Blease Road. Soon the road becomes a wide track heading along the
side of Blease Fell. There are some pretty streams and waterfalls to
watch out for along the way but be careful not to fall off the edge of
the loose surfaced track whilst watching them!

After about 2½ miles the track goes over a stile. Keep to the track
on the right close to the stone wall. Soon you will notice in the
distance Skiddaw House on the hillside in a clump of trees. The
house was once a row of shepherds' cottages but is now a youth
hostel. On arrival you have a choice of routes. You could go left for
a few yards then turn right onto a wide track which will take you to
Bassenthwaite village. Alternatively you could turn immediately
right at the stone wall and take the track downhill, eventually
meeting the River Caldew to Mosedale. On the right is Blencathra
and Bowscale Fell, on the left Pike and Carrock Fell. Fortunately if
you take the valley route you will avoid *mountaineering* biking!

Whichever route you choose the return route is on the road
through Mosedale and Mungrisdale if returning to Threlkeld. If
you started at Bassenthwaite and took the wide track to Skiddaw
House the return route would be via Mosedale then a long ride
round the edge of Caldbeck Fells passing near Hesket Newmarket,
Caldbeck and Longlands to return to Bassenthwaite.

There are many combinations using the routes around Skiddaw

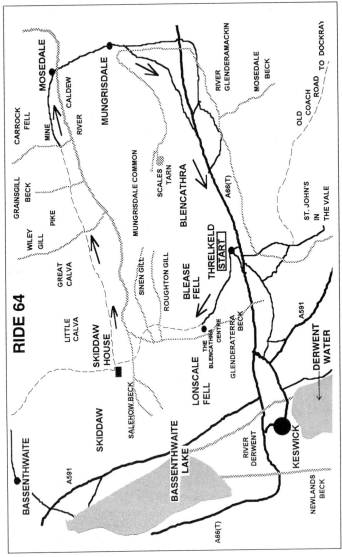

RIDE 64

MOSEDALE

MUNGRISDALE

CARROCK FELL

MINE

CALDEW

RIVER

GRAINSGILL BECK

WILEY GILL

PIKE

GREAT CALVA

LITTLE CALVA

SKIDDAW HOUSE

SINEN GILL

ROUGHTON GILL

MUNGRISDALE COMMON

SCALES TARN

BLENCATHRA

RIVER GLENDERAMACKIN

MOSEDALE BECK

OLD COACH ROAD TO DOCKRAY

A66(T)

ST. JOHN'S IN THE VALE

THRELKELD START

BLEASE FELL

THE BLENCATHRA CENTRE

GLENDERATERRA BECK

A591

SALEHOW BECK

LONSCALE FELL

SKIDDAW

A591

BASSENTHWAITE

BASSENTHWAITE LAKE

RIVER DERWENT

KESWICK

DERWENT WATER

NEWLANDS BECK

A66(T)

and Blencathra; I will leave it to you to decide how you wish to ride them. I have marked the most popular route on the map. Please bear in mind the extra mileage if you make your own route.

Whilst in the area you might like to try the old coach road which starts in St John's in the Vale and goes across Threlkeld Common to Dockray. It is an interesting ride of about 6 miles.

RIDE 65: BOOT - WASDALE HEAD - SANTON BRIDGE - DALEGARTH STATION

Fact File

Distance:	16 miles (26km)
Grading:	Only Tough Guys (and Gals) on this one!
Off Road:	35%
Start Grid Ref:	Dalegarth Station car park near Boot. OS Landranger 89/173008

Along the Way: After the hard ride over Eskdale Fell take time to rest along the bank of Wast Water and soak up the raw beauty of Wasdale. Wainwright described this area in his book of the southern fells as 'a bit of heaven fallen upon the earth'. How right he was.

Great Gable stands aloof at the head of the dale, commanding respect from all who dare venture onto its slopes.

On the left of Great Gable is Kirk Fell and on the right are the summits of Scafell and Scafell Pike, which at 3210ft is England's highest mountain. One day I will have to try the bridleway across to Sty Head. What a ride that would be!

The Route

Leave the car park at Dalegarth Station turning left, then in a few yards turn left again to Boot. Where the road ends continue over the bridge following the signs for bridleway, Burnmoor Tarn and Wasdale Head. Keep straight ahead through Eskdale Mill and up a stony track and through a gate. Bear right through the gate following the bridleway sign. The track climbs steeply over Eskdale Fell, past Burnmoor Tarn and bearing slightly to the left goes down to

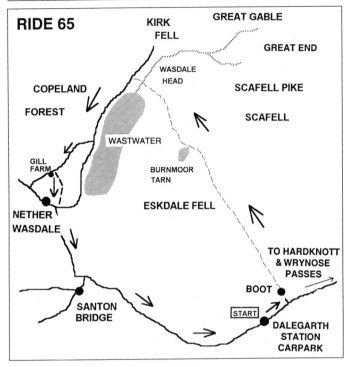

RIDE 65

KIRK FELL

GREAT GABLE

GREAT END

WASDALE HEAD

COPELAND FOREST

SCAFELL PIKE

SCAFELL

WASTWATER

GILL FARM

BURNMOOR TARN

NETHER WASDALE

ESKDALE FELL

TO HARDKNOTT & WRYNOSE PASSES

BOOT

SANTON BRIDGE

START

DALEGARTH STATION CARPARK

Wasdale Head car park. Go past the park and at the road turn left to ride alongside Wast Water. In 2½ miles follow the road around to the right signed to Gosforth. In about 1½ miles at Gill Farm follow the bridleway sign to the left following a wide track for 1 mile. At the road turn right then almost immediately left towards Santon Bridge. Keep following the Santon Bridge signs until you arrive at a 'T' junction. Turn left here signpost Eskdale. Follow the signs for Hardknott Pass and Boot to return to Eskdale Station.

RIDE 66: DENT CIRCULAR

Fact File

Distance:	11¹/₂ miles (18km)
Grading:	Moderate +
Off Road:	50%
Start Grid Ref:	Dent village car park. OS Outdoor Leisure 2. Yorkshire Dales Western Area. GR705870
Refreshments: both at Dent	The Sun Inn and The George and Dragon Hotel,

Along the Way: Dent village with its old houses and cobbled streets is worth exploring.

In the 17th and 18th centuries the 'terrible knitters o' Dent' held the key to Dent's prosperity. Wooden galleries were built onto the houses at first floor level where the knitters would clack their needles furiously. They knitted stockings and gloves mainly for the army.

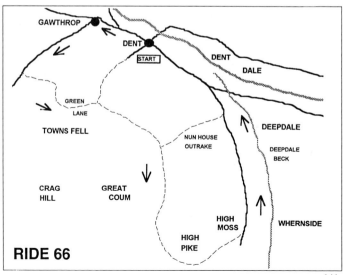

As with all labour intensive industries machinery took over and in the 19th-century Dent's fearsome knitters were doomed. A little further away is Dent railway station. It is the highest main line station in England and is part of the Settle - Carlisle line.

The Route

The suggested route as marked above starts and finishes at the Dent village car park. Turn right out of the park then in ¹/₂ mile turn left signposted to Barbon and Gawthrop. In Gawthrop village turn left at the bridge over Oliver Gill and start the steep climb up the Barbondale road. In a couple of miles look out for a wide track to the left signposted to Dent, Nun House and the end of the track, High Moss. It is a long, steady climb over Green Lane, which is the name of the track, and is quite stony in places. You will need all your mountain biking skills on this route!

In about 6 miles you arrive at High Moss and a narrow road. Turn left onto the road along Deepdale and left again at the junction at Howgill Bridge to return to your transport at Dent.

RIDE 67: THE WESTERN FORESTS

The forests with the Cumbrian mountains for a backdrop make ideal off road riding. Many have waymarked routes testing the skills of man and machine and most are open to riders to find their own routes, with due consideration for other forest users of course. Acknowledgement for these routes go to Forest Enterprise from whom leaflets are available from the visitor centre at Grizedale and Whinlatter, for which a small charge is made.

WHINLATTER FOREST PARK

Fact File

Distance:	Route 1 is 5 miles (8km) Route 2 is 7 miles (11km)
Grading:	Moderate
Off Road:	100%
Start Grid Ref:	Whinlatter Forest Park Visitor Centre. OS Landranger 89/209245

There are many routes in the Whinlatter Forest. Information is available from the visitor centre

The Whinlatter Forest Park is England's only mountain forest and has two waymarked cycle routes. A feature of the rides are the breathtaking views towards Grisedale Pike and Skiddaw. There is ample parking at the visitor centre which should be approached from the Whinlatter Pass.

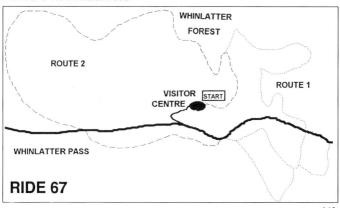

ENNERDALE FOREST is the largest area of woodland in West Cumbria being 6 miles in length, enclosing the beautiful River Liza that runs into Ennerdale Water. Although there are no waymarked routes in the forest the forest roads that climb towards Pillar and Chapel Crags are worthy of further exploration. Surrounded by some of the most rugged fells in Cumbria, with the aforementioned Pillar being the highest, it is supported by Kirk Fell, Steeple, Haycock, Hay Stacks and High Stile to mention but a few. Access to the forest is via Ennerdale Bridge.

BLENGDALE FOREST is a small forest west of Wast Water, its feature being some huge conifers. Not much to offer but a pleasant ride with car parking available alongside the River Bleng with its waterfall. Access from the A595 at Gosforth.

MITERDALE FOREST, a little south of Wast Water, is just off the A595 and is an area well worth exploring although there are no official cycle tracks. The forest is a mixture of conifers and broad-leaved trees making a contrast against each other. There is parking near the River Mite taking the road from Eskdale Green.

BROUGHTON MOOR FOREST is worth exploring if paying a visit to Coniston Water. It is only small but fairly rugged. Parking is available on the roadside between Torver and Broughton Mills. Between the trees it is possible to see across to the Duddon Estuary and the Dunnerdale Fells.

GRIZEDALE FOREST PARK offers over 10 miles of waymarked cycle tracks in the forest. A feature of the forest is its sculptures; a leaflet is available about the sculptures and cycle tracks at the visitor centre. There are ten car parking areas in this very popular forest which can become quite busy at times.

Grizedale Forest lies between Coniston Water and Windermere with Esthwaite Water snuggling to its northern boundary near Hawkshead. It can be approached from either Newby Bridge or Hawkshead.

RIDE 68: WHITEHAVEN TO ENNERDALE CYCLE TRACK

The path has been jointly promoted by the West Cumbria Groundwork Trust and Sustrans. The work was supported by Bardon Roadstone, BT, Copeland Borough Council, the Countryside Commission, Cumbria CC, the D of E, the Department of Trade & Industry, the European Development Fund and the Railway Ramblers, all of which helped with the funding of the project.

The cycle path uses part of an old railway track, made up paths and even an old tramway. The cycle path runs for 10 miles then minor roads must be used to complete the journey to arrive at the finish at Ennerdale Water. There are many access points but it is best to start from Whitehaven and have the beauty of the fells in front of you. Sculptures to watch out for along the way are freeform masonry walling, 40 seats, metal sculptural images, landscaping, seating and entrances.

A leaflet is available from the many information centres in the area.

RIDE 69: THE CUMBRIA CYCLE WAY

Although there is little off road riding on the Cumbria Cycle Way no book on cycling in the Lake District would be complete without mentioning this grand tour of 259 miles (417km) around the Cumbrian countryside. The route is divided into 7 sections varying in length from a lazy 27 miles to a more energetic 46 miles.

The cycle way follows the coast from Carlisle through Maryport and Whitehaven to Arnside, veering inland to Kirkby Lonsdale then north via Kirkby Stephen and Brampton to return to Carlisle. It is an interesting alternative to the more traditional routes which pass through the heart of Lakeland. There is a Buddhist study centre near Ulverston, Muncaster Castle, 'Laal Ratty' at Ravenglass, Furness Abbey and many more historic and interesting attractions along the way. A well laid out leaflet showing the route and listing places of interest, visitor centres and camping sites is available from most tourist information centres, or a fuller description is found in *The Cumbria Cycle Way* by Roy Walker and Ron Jarvis (Cicerone).

CHAPTER 10
Cheshire & Lancashire

CHESHIRE

RIDE 70: THE MIDDLEWOOD WAY

The Middlewood Way is a joint user track and it is requested that everyone uses the facility sensitively and with due consideration for each other. Cyclists must use the bridlepath where possible and on shared sections should give way to pedestrians at all times.

MACCLESFIELD TO MARPLE

Fact File

Distance:	11 miles (18km)
Grading:	Easy
Off Road:	100%
Start Grid Ref:	Macclesfield. OS Landranger 118/918745. There are various access points along the way with car parks or lay-bys at Rose Hill Station, Marple, High Lane, Higher Poynton, Bollington and Macclesfield.

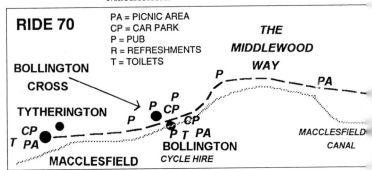

Refreshments:　　Pubs and cafes at various points. (See map for guide)

Along the Way:　　The Macclesfield Canal, views across to the Peak District, the wildlife, and the remains of the industrial heritage

History:　　The railway and canal were built to link the area with Stockport for the transportation of coal, stone, cotton and silk. There were stone quarries, cotton mills and coal mines nearby providing much needed employment for the men in the district. The remains of many of the abandoned mine shafts still scar the countryside. Whilst some of the old cotton mills have become derelict, others have been converted for modern business use. Stone quarries still exist in the area supplying local stone for building or ornamental utilisation.

Acknowledgement: Macclesfield Borough Council, Stockport Metropolitan Borough Council, the Countryside Commission

The Route

Whilst riding the Middlewood Way it is easy to imagine a goods train slogging its way to the mills laden with coal from one of the local pits, or a passenger train carrying a party of holidaymakers to the coast. The smell of steam and smoke alas is no more as we join the Middlewood Way for a peaceful ride on the bed of the old railway line.

There are many access points on the Middlewood Way as it winds alongside the Macclesfield Canal. Picnic areas abound and there are refreshments available at Wood Lanes and at the many

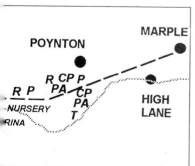

pubs in the district. Watch the boats gliding along the Macclesfield Canal, carrying tourists today instead of the bales of 19th-century cotton of yesteryear. Linger awhile to enjoy the views across to the Peak District in the distance.

Don't hurry as you travel along this well laid out track; take the time to stop occasionally and absorb the beauty of the area.

147

The observant will revel in the abundant wildlife on the Middlewood Way, perhaps catching a glimpse of a grey squirrel or if you care to ride early morning you might see a fox returning to its earth after a night of scavenging for food. Whatever you do, enjoy riding this part of Cheshire which once bustled with industrial activity and has now become part of our industrial heritage.

LANCASHIRE

> ### RIDE 71: LEVER PARK - RIVINGTON RESERVOIR - RIVINGTON PIKE

Fact File

Distance:	5 miles (8km)
Grading:	Easy, but climbs to 1191ft.
Off Road:	95%
Start Grid Ref:	Lever Park. Choose your own starting point from the car parks marked on the route. Lever Park GR 109/630138

Refreshments: The old Cruck Barns in Lever Park provide refreshment facilities.

Along the Way: Rivington Pike, the Barns, Liverpool Castle, Rivington Hall and the Rivington Terraced Gardens. Leaflets on all these attractions are available in the park at the tourist information centre.

History: Lever Park was given to the people of Bolton in 1902 by W.H. Lever who later became Lord Leverhulme. It is beautifully landscaped with tree-lined avenues.

The Rivington Terraced Gardens on a site below Rivington Pike were developed in the early 1900s. A bungalow was built on the site along with three entrance lodges. The gardens were laid out in 1905 and the magnificent Pigeon Tower was built in 1910. A ravine with waterfalls, rock pools and terraces was built; there was even a Japanese Garden. Unfortunately the gardens and buildings became neglected and after the second world war the bungalow and lodges

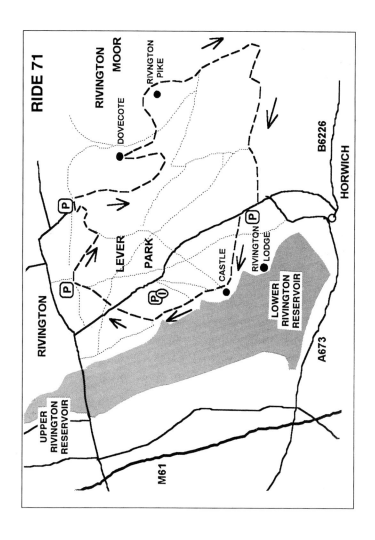

The gate of Liverpool Castle with Rivington Pike in the distance

were demolished. The gardens are now open to the public and have been partially renovated.

The Barns in the park are 17th-century Cruck framed and are now used for refreshments and information centres. Liverpool Castle on the shore of the reservoir is a replica of the original castle; not as a complete building but built as a ruin. The intention was to rebuild it as it would have appeared after the civil war.

Rivington Pike is on an old beacon site on the western edge of the West Pennine Moors. The Pike Tower was built in 1733 and some of the original stone from the old beacon was used in its construction. It is now owned by Chorley District Council and is a Grade 2 Listed Building. Various events are held at the Pike, including a fair which is held on Good Friday and the annual Pike Race held on Easter Saturday.

Acknowledgement: North West Water, Lancashire CC, West Pennine Moors Information Service

The Route
Please keep to the route as marked for this 5 mile circular to Rivington Pike. You can start at any of the car parks and cycle in either direction; the arrows on the map are there simply for guidance. A more detailed route card is available from the information centre in the park.

RIDE 72: THE RIVINGTON & YARROW RESERVOIRS

Fact File

Distance:	7¹/₂ miles (12km)
Grading:	Easy
Off Road:	95%
Start Grid Ref:	Lever Park. Choose your own starting point from the car parks marked on the route. Lever Park GR 109/630138

Refreshments, Along the Way, and *History* are the same as for Route 1.

The Route

This is a 7$^{1}/_2$ mile route along the side of the Rivington and Yarrow reservoirs. Please keep to the marked route, if more detail is required a route card is available from the information centre in the park. The arrows suggest the direction of travel but you may cycle in the opposite direction if you wish.

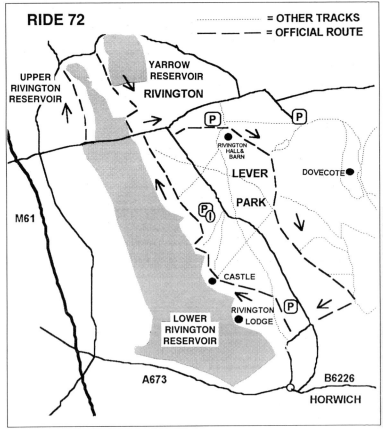

RIDE 73: ROUTES AROUND LANCASTER

Lancaster makes use of disused railway tracks between Lancaster and Glasson, south towards Fishnet Point. An easterly route takes you past Halton, and a westerly route to Morecambe on the coast. There is an excellent leaflet describing these routes available from the Lancashire County Council and titled *River Lune Recreational Footpaths & Cycleways* and they can all be accessed in Lancaster near to where the existing British Rail line crosses the River Lune. The track to Glasson starts a little further south but a connecting road can be picked up near the river. There is also a 'quiet road' route called the University Route for which a leaflet is available from Lancashire CC which makes cycling safer when riding between city and university.

Proposed Great Harwood to Blackburn Cycleway
A short part of this proposed off road cycle route is available between Great Harwood and Lower Cunliffe where the track ends. It uses the disused railway for 3 miles. Eventually a track will be opened to take you all the way into Blackburn.

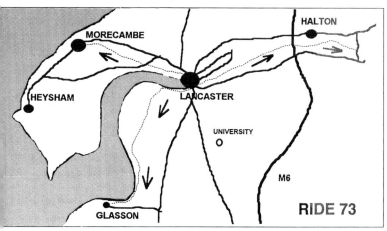

RIDE 74: GISBURN FOREST

This wild and undulating forest contains roads and tracks to suit all abilities of rider. There are two car parks close to the Stocks Reservoir and views over the Forest of Bowland. There are no waymarked tracks but the forest is open for cyclists to explore.

RIDE 75: THE LEEDS - LIVERPOOL CANAL
WIGAN - BURSCOUGH CANAL PATH

Fact File

Distance: 11 miles (18km)

Grading: Easy

Off Road: 100%

Start Grid Ref: Wigan Pier. OS Landranger 108/576053

Refreshments: Numerous pubs serving food and drink within easy reach of the towpath

Along the Way: Martin Mere Wildfowl Reserve, Beacon Country Park, Rufford Old Hall, Wigan Pier, Pennington Flash Country Park, and the Haigh Country Park are all within a short cycling distance of the Canal.

History: The Wigan - Burscough canal path is part of the Leeds - Liverpool Canal which is 127 miles long, being the longest single canal in the country. It took 46 years to build and was completed in 1816.

It was financially successful, transporting cotton from the Port of Liverpool to the mills further east. It passes through beautiful scenery as it crosses the Pennine Chain.

Acknowledgement: British Waterways, Countryside Commission, Transport & Road Research Laboratory

The Route
This experimental route for cyclists, walkers and anglers is provided
154

by British Waterways Leisure, permit free. It has easy access at Wigan Pier and finishes near Burscough. There is a choice of return routes either on the towpath or by road. There are many link roads to the towpath and the Lancashire Cycleway meets it near Appleby Bridge. The route passes through beautiful scenery and is close to many other attractions. There are three country parks and a wildfowl park within easy reach. Rufford Old Hall and the Wigan Pier Heritage Centre are worth a visit for their historical interest.

British Waterways request riders to respect the following:

- Keep to the left
- Do not obstruct the towpath
- Dismount at bridges, gates and pavements
- Slow down when approaching pedestrians
- Give warning of your approach
- Do not use linking footpaths
- Adhere to British Waterways by-laws
- No swimming in the canal
- Leave no litter
- Follow the country code

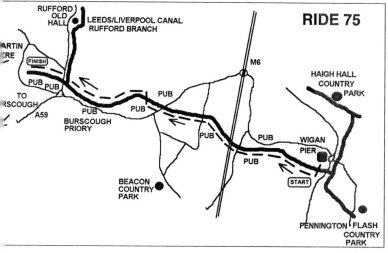

CHAPTER 11

South Tyneside & Northumberland

SOUTH TYNESIDE

RIDE 76: THE RIVER DON ROUTE

Fact File

Distance:	9 miles (15km)
Grading:	Easy
Off Road:	80%
Start Grid Ref:	Jarrow, car park near Bede Monastery Museum. OS Landranger 88/338655

Refreshments: The Bede Monastery Museum cafe. The Robin Hood pub adjacent to the A194

Along the Way: The Bede Monastery Museum at the start is in the 18th-century Jarrow Hall and tells the story of the Anglo-Saxon and medieval monastic site of St Paul's, Jarrow that was the home of the Venerable Bede.

Visit St Paul's Church and the remains of the old monastery which dates back to AD 681 that is close by.

The Bede Gallery at Monkton has items of interest on the Jarrow march and shipyards as well as exhibitions by local and national artists. Near the gallery is the Primrose Nature Reserve and Mill Dene Town Farm.

JARROW HALL
(BEDE MONASTER
MUSEUM)

ST. PAUL'S
CHURCH

Acknowledgement: South Tyneside Metropolitan Borough Council

The Route

Start at Jarrow Hall and pay a visit to the Bede Monastery Museum. Ride down to where the River

Don flows into the Tyne. This is wildlife habitat for waterfowl and wading birds. Follow the Don upstream to arrive at St Paul's Church and ruins. Continue upstream with the church on your right until you meet a bridge; you can take either bank now to go under the dual carriageway then across the field to the Metro line bridge that crosses the A19.

Go under the Metro line and immediately turn left then after a few yards turn right to follow a path under the A19 to a footbridge. Take the main footpath on the left bank of the Don that leads to a road, cross carefully and re-join the Don footpath. Keep on upstream to another footbridge and cross over. On the left is Primrose Nature Reserve and Mill Dene Town Farm. If you wish to visit the Bede Gallery you must take the footpath on the right alongside the Monkton Burn into Springwell Park where the gallery is situated.

Back at the River Don continue upstream and stop for a breather at the Robin Hood pub just off Leam Lane. If you wish to visit the remains of Boldon Watermill go under Leam Lane and follow the river as far as Hedworth Lane, Thorntree Walk and Hedworth Dene and the A19. Look for the footbridge to cross the A19 and return to the Don path that leads to Boldon Colliery, passing the remains of Boldon Watermill on the right.

The South Tyneside MBC recommend that cyclists do not go any further along this route and it would be wise to respect their wishes.

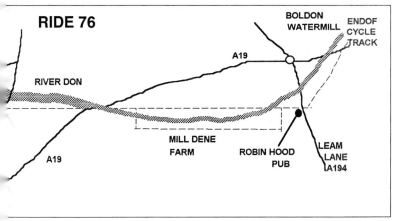

Retrace your tracks to the footbridge just north of the Robin Hood and make your return to Jarrow more interesting by riding along the opposite bank of the River Don.

RIDE 77: THE MONKTON MINERAL LINE CYCLEWAY

Fact File

Distance:	2 miles (3km)
Grading:	Easy
Off Road:	100%
Start Grid Ref:	Monkton Lane. OS Landranger 88/316629
History:	The route takes the disused Mineral Line.
Acknowledgement:	South Tyneside Metropolitan Borough Council

The Route
This route, although short, could be used to link up with the Hebburn Cycleway and thus merits inclusion. It starts at Monkton Lane to join the old rail track through Monkton village. It then goes north along the former mineral line to cross Albert Road to the interchange with Beech Street and St Oswald's Road. This is as far as the route goes at present and you should leave the track here. You must not travel any further north as you would be trespassing.

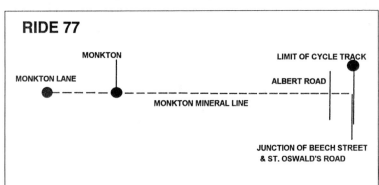

158

RIDE 78: THE HEBBURN CYCLEWAY

Fact File

Distance:	3¹/₂ miles (5km)
Grading:	Easy
Off Road:	30%
Start Grid Ref:	Hebburn. OS Landranger 88/300634
Acknowledgement:	South Tyneside Metropolitan Borough Council

The Route

Another short route but easily linked to the other two rides alongside the River Tyne on the official cycle route. It passes through Hebburn Riverside Park to emerge at Consort Road. It picks up the River Tyne Cycle Route and continues left into Lyons Street as far as Waggonway Road, Blackett Street and Western Road.

A circular route could be used at the rider's discretion using the River Don path, then cutting across to the Monkton Mineral Line rejoining the Hebburn to return in the opposite direction.

NORTHUMBERLAND

RIDE 79: DERWENT RESERVOIR & SLALEY FOREST

Fact File

Distance:	16 miles (25km)
Grading:	Moderate
Off Road:	20%
Start Grid Ref:	Blanchland. OS Landranger 87/965504
Refreshments:	The Lord Crewe pub at Blanchland
Along the Way:	The Derwent Reservoir caters for anglers, power

boats and yachting and there are many picnic places along its shores to rest your weary limbs. On the final run down to Blanchland past

Pennypie House watch out for the remains of Shildon Mine which is thought to be one of the oldest mines in the area. You will see the ruins of the old engine house standing proud on the right. It is built in the style of Cornish mining buildings and is said to be the only one left in northern England.

The Route
Leave the car park in Blanchland turning right and at the village centre take the road signposted to the Derwent Reservoir. In 1$\frac{1}{2}$ miles turn left at the sign for the Carrick Picnic Area. This quiet road takes you along the side of the Derwent Reservoir ending at a 'T' junction 4$\frac{1}{2}$ miles further along. Turn left here signposted to Blanchland and Slaley. Keep following the signs for Slaley and in half a mile bear right. At the crossroads turn left signposted to Blanchland and Dukesfield. At the next crossroads go straight on following the sign to Ladycross then at yet another crossroads go left into Slaley Forest. When the tarmac road peters out continue straight ahead along the forest road. Soon you arrive at a gate leading onto Blanchland Moor; follow the bridleway sign along a wide track over the moor. It is hard going uphill, especially if wet, but your reward will be the thrill of the downhill section. Keep straight ahead following a wide but rough track and eventually leave the moor through a gate. The track goes downhill to a junction at the bottom. You have a choice now, either to take the easy way out and turn left through the gate to return to Blanchland and the car park or to bear right over the moor to Baybridge, turning left at the road for Blanchland.

The following three routes offer a flavour of Northumberland around Hexamshire Common. They start and finish at Whitley Chapel and each route has its own character and presents the challenge of the common in a different way. It would be advisable to take the appropriate Ordnance Survey map with you and make sure that you are well prepared for traversing open moorland.

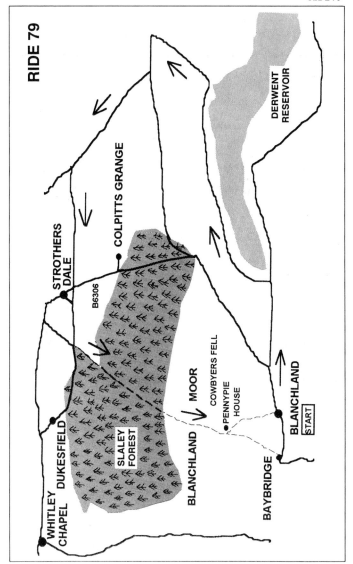

RIDE 79

DERWENT RESERVOIR

STROTHERS DALE

COLPITTS GRANGE

B6306

SLALEY FOREST

COWBYERS FELL

PENNYPIE HOUSE

BLANCHLAND MOOR

BLANCHLAND
START

BAYBRIDGE

WHITLEY CHAPEL

DUKESFIELD

RIDE 80: THE DRAG

Fact File

Distance:	7 miles (11km)
Grading:	Easy (moderate if wet along 'The Drag')
Off Road:	23%
Start Grid Ref:	Whitley Chapel. OS Landranger 87/928578
Refreshments:	The Fox & Hounds Inn at Whitley Chapel

Along the Way: This ride has a wild beauty all of its own on the edge of Hexamshire Common. The views across to Burntridge Moor, Bulbeck Common and Embley Fell are so rewarding. The off road section is a permissive bridleway called 'The Drag'. It was built to assist in timber extraction in the area earlier this century.

The Route

There is parking for a few cars on the grass verge near the crossroads in Whitley Chapel. Leave in a westerly direction towards Dalton then in a few hundred yards take the left fork in the direction of Burnt Ridge. This is a very quiet road linking farms together. After about 1¼ miles look out for a track rising off to the left through a

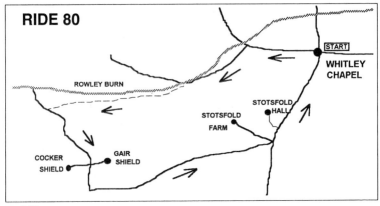

RIDE 80

ROWLEY BURN

START

WHITLEY
CHAPEL

STOTSFOLD
HALL

STOTSFOLD
FARM

COCKER
SHIELD

GAIR
SHIELD

gate. On the gate post you will see a map and the history of this permissive bridleway. Ride the track until it meets a minor road then turn left for a hard slog up the steep hill. Eventually you join another minor road; take care at this junction and go left to enjoy a pleasant downhill ride to return to Whitley Chapel.

RIDE 81: THE BURNT RIDGE CHALLENGE

Fact File

Distance:	16 miles (25km)
Grading:	Rough and Tough. Some navigational skills may be required
Off Road:	50%
Start Grid Ref:	Whitley Chapel. OS Landranger 87/928578
Refreshments:	The Fox & Hounds Inn at Whitley Chapel. Various facilities in Allendale Town
Along the Way:	Scenery is the best part of this ride with magnificent views across the moors in all directions.

The Route

You can start at Whitley Chapel or Allendale Town. If starting from Whitley Chapel take the road towards Dalton in a westerly direction and in a few hundred yards take the minor road on the left. Follow this until you cross a stream; watch out for wet feet! Continue straight ahead along a rocky track to join a bridleway onto the moor through a gate in about a mile. Follow this rough bridleway over the moor in a south westerly direction for 3 miles to join the road. Turn right at the junction to Allendale Town.

Turn right again in Allendale then immediately after a sharp left bend turn right up a narrow road to Moorhouse Gate. The road climbs steeply to a farm which is on a double bend. Immediately after the farm buildings turn right onto a wide track, a byway, which leads to the public bridleway to take you across the edge of Eshells Moor to the road at High Eshells. Follow the road to Dalton and Whitley Chapel.

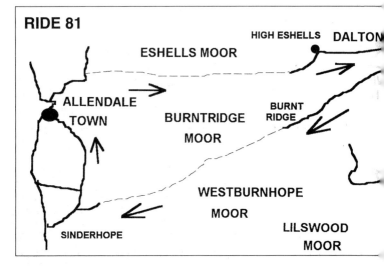

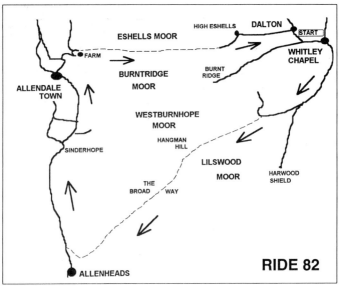

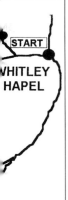

The track from Lilswood Moor

RIDE 82: THE BROAD WAY ROUTE

Fact File

Distance:	21 miles (31km)
Grading:	Rough and Tough. Some navigational skills may be required
Off Road:	50%
Start Grid Ref:	Whitley Chapel. OS Landranger 87/928578

Refreshments: The Fox & Hounds Inn at Whitley Chapel. Various facilities in Allendale Town

Along the Way: The Broad Way is an old trail which was used by horses to transport lead to the smelt mills at Dukesfield. Where it crosses a junction of tracks at Hangman Hill there was probably a gibbet many years ago.

The Route
Once again the route starts at Whitley Chapel but this time leave in a southerly direction keeping the church on your left. After a long uphill slog of about two miles take the narrow road right towards Westburnhope. After crossing the cattle grid the road turns sharp right; your route is straight ahead onto the moor along a wide track. In a few yards the wide track bears left. Ignore this and go straight ahead over some rough soil and look for a narrow track through the heather. In a few yards a bridleway post confirms your route. The track now heads over Lilswood Moor to a junction of tracks at Hangman Hill. Make sure you take the right bridleway here which continues south along Broad Way over Tedham Moss to emerge onto the B6295 at Fell View. Turn right here and head north to Allendale Town. Continue straight on through the town and after a sharp left bend turn right up a narrow road to Moorhouse Gate. The road climbs steeply to a farm which is on a double bend. Immediately after the farm buildings turn right onto a wide track, a byway, which leads to the public bridleway to take you across the edge of Eshells Moor to the road at High Eshells. Follow the road through Dalton to return to Whitley Chapel.

RIDE 83: KIELDER FOREST

Fabulous Kielder! This is northern Europe's largest man-made lake which is set in Europe's largest man-made forest. It takes its name from the Kielder Burn which means violent water. The forest is awash with wildlife with heron and osprey breeding at Bakethin.

There are ample opportunities for cyclists to ride the forest tracks. Unfortunately, as far as this book is concerned I am unable to publish the routes as they are constantly updated or completely changed on a three year cycle to fit in with timber felling operations.

Kielder Bikes have a cycle hire centre at the Hawkhope car park alongside the lake near the dam. They will advise you on the cycle routes which are currently available. Alternatively Forest Enterprise regularly publish a leaflet on cycle routes and they can be contacted at Eals Burn, Bellingham, Hexham NE48 2AJ. The visitor centre at Tower Knowe may also be able to give advice.

RIDE 84: SIX DAYS OF RIDING AROUND HADRIAN'S WALL AND NORTHUMBERLAND

This route was devised and kindly donated by the Youth Hostel Association and there is a hostel at the end of each day's ride. The route follows Hadrian's Wall and has a good historic content with Roman relics scattered all over the place. The route is totally on the road but for anyone wishing to explore the Hadrian's Wall area I include the route in the book for your consideration.

CARLISLE - ACOMB - CARLISLE

Fact File

Distance:	146 or 153 miles (225 or 236km)
Grading:	Easy
Off Road:	None
Start Grid Ref:	Carlisle YHA. OS Landranger 85/386569

Refreshments: The route passes through many villages where there are cafes and pubs.

Along the Way: The main feature of this ride is Hadrian's Wall and the Roman occupation. Allow time to visit the forts and museums and be prepared to pay a small charge at some of the sites.

History: The whole area is bursting with historical interest, especially in connection with the Romans. I suggest you purchase a guide to the Roman Wall before leaving Carlisle and clue yourself up on the history.

167

The Route
Day 1 - Carlisle
It would be a good idea to spend day 1 in Carlisle and if you are staying at the hostel please arrive after 5pm; there is an evening meal at 7pm if required. Carlisle is an interesting place to explore with its castle and cathedral and has all the cafes and pubs you could desire.

Day 2 - Carlisle to Greenhead, 21 miles
A short run today to get you into the swing of things, just 21 miles. From the hostel go to the A7 turning right then left along the B6264 to Brampton which is about 7 miles; morning coffee could be taken here. Leave Brampton on the A69 east and after about ¹/₂ mile turn left to Lanercost where there is a priory and church. Turn right at the junction and in 1 mile go left to Banks then follow Hadrian's Wall to Birdoswald and its fort. Continue along the B6318 to Gilsland where refreshment may be taken if required, then on to Greenhead and visit the Roman Army Museum and Walltown Craggs and on to the YHA.

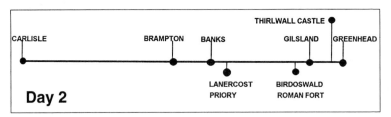

Day 3 - Greenhead to Acomb, 22 miles
Follow the B6318 east to Once Brewed/Twice Brewed. There is a cafe and a pub here as well as a National Parks Information Centre. Turn left to the car park where a walk on the wall has superb views of Crag Lough. Return to the B6318 and in a short way turn left to Housesteads Roman Fort where refreshments are available. Return to the B6318 then have a look at Chesters Roman Fort 8 miles away. Continue along the B6318 to Chollerford and go right over the river then right at the crossroads onto the A6079 for 2¹/₂ miles then go left signposted to Acomb. If you wish to stay at the Acomb Hostel it may

be necessary to obtain the key from the warden's house. There are no meals available at this hostel.

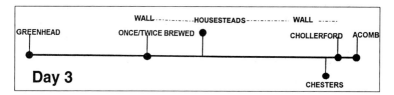

Day 4 - Acomb to Acomb, 21 or 30 miles
Turn right leaving the hostel then right again to Fallowfield. Continue through Fallowfield to the B6318. Turn left here then in about $2^1/2$ miles cross the A6079 and eventually take the B6320 to Wark.

For the fittest a fine ride north by the side of the River North Tyne to Bellingham for lunch is an option here. The return trip adds about 10 miles to the day's ride.

From Wark cross the river and take the road past Chipchase Castle and Gardens to Barrasford. From here continue to the A6079, turn right and return to Acomb. If you have any energy left a visit to Hexham is a must.

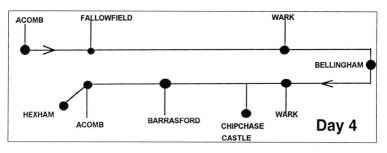

Day 5 - Acomb to Edmundbyers, 20 miles
A short run today after yesterday's exersions! Leave Acomb taking the minor road to Oakwood and Anick crossing under the A69 to reach Corbridge. After searching out the Roman Fort remains leave Corbridge over the River Tyne, cross the A695 to join the B6307 and

eventually the B6306 at Dipton Wood and continue along turning left into Slaley where a little light refreshment may be taken in the local pub.

Suitably refreshed pass through Slaley and turn right across the Kellas Plantation. Continue along to join the A68 then turn right, turning right again at the B6278 to Edmundbyers. If you have time a detour to the Derwent Reservoir would be rewarding.

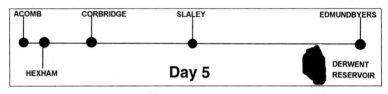

Day 6 - Edmundbyers to Once Brewed, 31 miles

From the Edmundbyers Hostel take the B6306 to Blanchland then continue on for 9 miles to the outskirts of Hexham. Turn left for the racecourse and in 4 miles go left onto the B6305 eventually joining the A686. Turn right then first left and navigate on minor roads northwards to reach Bardon Mill. On the way visit Ridley Hall and Beltingham then cross the river by footbridge to Bardon Mill. From here pick up the signs for the Vindola Roman Fort and on to Once Brewed.

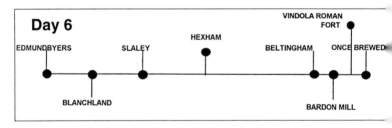

Day 7 - Once Brewed to Carlisle, 31 miles

From the Once Brewed Hostel head south on minor roads towards the A69. Go straight across then turn right and head for Haltwhistle. Leave Haltwhistle in a southerly direction to the A69 which you

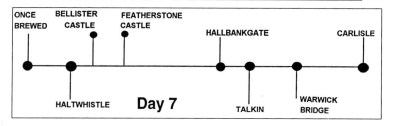

must cross again, then cross the river and head along past the remains of Bellister Castle to Broomhouse, Featherstone Castle eventually joining the A689. Go right onto the A689 towards Brampton and Hallbankgate then left to Talkin and Warwick Bridge where the weary may rest and sample the brew. Cross the A69 to Newby East and join the B6264 and back to Carlisle.

CICERONE GUIDES

Cicerone publish a wide range of reliable guides to walking and climbing abroad

FRANCE, BELGIUM & LUXEMBOURG
CHAMONIX MONT BLANC - A Walking Guide
THE CORSICAN HIGH LEVEL ROUTE: GR20
FRENCH ROCK
THE PYRENEAN TRAIL: GR10
THE RLS (Stevenson) TRAIL
ROCK CLIMBS IN BELGIUM & LUXEMBOURG
ROCK CLIMBS IN THE VERDON
TOUR OF MONT BLANC
TOUR OF THE OISANS: GR54
TOUR OF THE QUEYRAS
WALKING THE FRENCH ALPS: GR5
WALKING THE FRENCH GORGES (Provence)
WALKS IN VOLCANO COUNTRY (Auvergne)
THE WAY OF ST JAMES: GR65

FRANCE / SPAIN
WALKS AND CLIMBS IN THE PYRENEES
ROCK CLIMBS IN THE PYRENEES

SPAIN & PORTUGAL
ANDALUSIAN ROCK CLIMBS
BIRDWATCHING IN MALLORCA
COSTA BLANCA CLIMBS
MOUNTAIN WALKS ON THE COSTA BLANCA
WALKING IN MALLORCA
WALKS & CLIMBS IN THE PICOS DE EUROPA
THE WAY OF ST JAMES: SPAIN
WALKING IN THE ALGARVE

FRANCE / SWITZERLAND
CHAMONIX TO ZERMATT The Walker's Haute Route
THE JURA - Walking the High Route and Winter Ski
    Traverses

SWITZERLAND
THE ALPINE PASS ROUTE
THE BERNESE ALPS
CENTRAL SWITZERLAND
THE GRAND TOUR OF MONTE ROSA (inc Italy)
WALKS IN THE ENGADINE
WALKING IN TICINO
THE VALAIS - A Walking Guide

GERMANY / AUSTRIA / EASTERN EUROPE
HUT-TO-HUT IN THE STUBAI ALPS
THE HIGH TATRAS
THE KALKALPEN TRAVERSE
KING LUDWIG WAY
KLETTERSTEIG - Scrambles
MOUNTAIN WALKING IN AUSTRIA
WALKING IN THE BLACK FOREST
WALKING IN THE HARZ MOUNTAINS
WALKING IN THE SALZKAMMERGUT

ITALY & SLOVENIA
ALTA VIA - High Level Walks in the Dolomites
CLASSIC CLIMBS IN THE DOLOMITES
THE GRAND TOUR OF MONTE ROSA inc Switzerland))
ITALIAN ROCK - Rock Climbs in Northern Italy
VIA FERRATA - Scrambles in the Dolomites
WALKING IN THE DOLOMITES
WALKS IN THE JULIAN ALPS

MEDITERRANEAN COUNTRIES
THE ATLAS MOUNTAINS
CRETE: Off the beaten track
THE MOUNTAINS OF GREECE
THE MOUNTAINS OF TURKEY
TREKS & CLIMBS IN WADI RUM, JORDAN
THE ALA DAG - Climbs & Treks (Turkey)

OTHER COUNTRIES
ADVENTURE TREKS - W. N. AMERICA
ANNAPURNA TREKKERS GUIDE
CLASSIC TRAMPS IN NEW ZEALAND
MOUNTAIN WALKING IN AFRICA 1: KENYA
ROCK CLIMBS IN HONG KONG
TREKKING IN THE CAUCAUSUS
TREKKING IN NEPAL
TREKKING - WESTERN NORTH AMERICA

GENERAL OUTDOOR BOOKS
THE ADVENTURE ALTERNATIVE
FAMILY CAMPING
FIRST AID FOR HILLWALKERS
THE HILL WALKERS MANUAL
LIMESTONE -100 BEST CLIMBS IN BRITAIN
MOUNTAIN WEATHER
MOUNTAINEERING LITERATURE
MODERN ALPINE CLIMBING
MODERN SNOW & ICE TECHNIQUES
ROPE TECHNIQUES IN MOUNTAINEERING

CANOEING
CANOEIST'S GUIDE TO THE NORTH EAST
SNOWDONIA WILD WATER, SEA & SURF
WILDWATER CANOEING

CARTOON BOOKS
ON FOOT & FINGER
ON MORE FEET & FINGERS
LAUGHS ALONG THE PENNINE WAY
THE WALKERS

*Also a full range of guidebooks
to walking, scrambling, ice-climbing,
rock climbing, and other adventurous
pursuits in Britain and abroad*

---

*Other guides are constantly being added to the Cicerone List.
Available from bookshops, outdoor equipment shops or direct (send for price list)
from CICERONE, 2 POLICE SQUARE, MILNTHORPE, CUMBRIA, LA7 7PY*

CICERONE GUIDES
Cicerone publish a wide range of reliable guides to walking and climbing in Britain, and other general interest books.

LAKE DISTRICT - General Books
CONISTON COPPER A History
CHRONICLES OF MILNTHORPE
A DREAM OF EDEN
THE HIGH FELLS OF LAKELAND
LAKELAND - A taste to remember (Recipes)
LAKELAND VILLAGES
LAKELAND TOWNS
THE LOST RESORT? (Morecambe)
LOST LANCASHIRE (Furness area)
OUR CUMBRIA Stories of Cumbrian Men and Women
THE PRIORY OF CARTMEL
REFLECTIONS ON THE LAKES
AN ILLUSTRATED COMPANION INTO LAKELAND

LAKE DISTRICT - Guide Books
THE BORDERS OF LAKELAND
BIRDS OF MORECAMBE BAY
CASTLES IN CUMBRIA
CONISTON COPPER MINES Field Guide
THE CUMBRIA CYCLE WAY
THE EDEN WAY
IN SEARCH OF WESTMORLAND
SHORT WALKS IN LAKELND-1: SOUTH LAKELAND
SCRAMBLES IN THE LAKE DISTRICT
MORE SCRAMBLES IN THE LAKE DISTRICT
WALKING ROUND THE LAKES
WALKS IN SILVERDALE/ARNSIDE
WESTMORLAND HERITAGE WALK
WINTER CLIMBS IN THE LAKE DISTRICT

NORTHERN ENGLAND (outside the Lakes
BIRDWATCHING ON MERSEYSIDE
CANAL WALKS Vol 1 North
CANOEISTS GUIDE TO THE NORTH EAST
THE CLEVELAND WAY & MISSING LINK
THE DALES WAY
DOUGLAS VALLEY WAY
WALKING IN THE FOREST OF BOWLAND
HADRIANS WALL Vol 1 The Wall Walk
HERITAGE TRAILS IN NW ENGLAND
THE ISLE OF MAN COASTAL PATH
IVORY TOWERS & DRESSED STONES (Follies)
THE LANCASTER CANAL
LANCASTER CANAL WALKS
A WALKERS GUIDE TO THE LANCASTER CANAL
LAUGHS ALONG THE PENNINE WAY
A NORTHERN COAST-TO-COAST
NORTH YORK MOORS Walks
THE REIVERS WAY (Northumberland)
THE RIBBLE WAY
ROCK CLIMBS LANCASHIRE & NW
WALKING DOWN THE LUNE
WALKING IN THE SOUTH PENNINES
WALKING IN THE NORTH PENNINES
WALKING IN THE WOLDS
WALKS IN THE YORKSHIRE DALES (3 VOL)
WALKS IN LANCASHIRE WITCH COUNTRY
WALKS IN THE NORTH YORK MOORS
WALKS TO YORKSHIRE WATERFALLS (2 vol)
WATERFALL WALKS -TEESDALE & THE HIGH PENNINES
WALKS ON THE WEST PENNINE MOORS
WALKING NORTHERN RAILWAYS (2 vol)
THE YORKSHIRE DALES A walker's guide

Also a full range of EUROPEAN and OVERSEAS guidebooks - walking, long distance trails, scrambling, ice-climbing, rock climbing.

DERBYSHIRE & EAST MIDLANDS
KINDER LOG
HIGH PEAK WALKS
WHITE PEAK WALKS
WHITE PEAK WALKS - 2 Vols
WEEKEND WALKS IN THE PEAK DISTRICT
THE VIKING WAY
THE DEVIL'S MILL / WHISTLING CLOUGH (Novels)

WALES & WEST MIDLANDS
ASCENT OF SNOWDON
WALKING IN CHESHIRE
CLWYD ROCK
HEREFORD & THE WYE VALLEY A Walker's Guide
HILLWALKING IN SNOWDONIA
HILL WALKING IN WALES (2 Vols)
THE MOUNTAINS OF ENGLAND & WALES Vol 1 WALES
WALKING OFFA'S DYKE PATH
THE RIDGES OF SNOWDONIA
ROCK CLIMBS IN WEST MIDLANDS
SARN HELEN Walking Roman Road
SCRAMBLES IN SNOWDONIA
SNOWDONIA WHITE WATER SEA & SURF
THE SHROPSHIRE HILLS A Walker's Guide
WALKING DOWN THE WYE
WELSH WINTER CLIMBS

SOUTH & SOUTH WEST ENGLAND
WALKING IN THE CHILTERNS
COTSWOLD WAY
COTSWOLD WALKS (3 VOLS)
WALKING ON DARTMOOR
WALKERS GUIDE TO DARTMOOR PUBS
EXMOOR & THE QUANTOCKS
THE KENNET & AVON WALK
LONDON THEME WALKS
AN OXBRIDGE WALK
A SOUTHERN COUNTIES BIKE GUIDE
THE SOUTHERN-COAST-TO-COAST
SOUTH DOWNS WAY & DOWNS LINK
SOUTH WEST WAY - 2 Vol
THE TWO MOORS WAY Dartmoor-Exmoor
WALKS IN KENT Bk 2
THE WEALDWAY & VANGUARD WAY

SCOTLAND
THE BORDER COUNTRY - WALKERS GUIDE
BORDER PUBS & INNS A Walker's Guide
CAIRNGORMS WINTER CLIMBS
WALKING THE GALLOWAY HILLS
THE ISLAND OF RHUM
THE SCOTTISH GLENS (Mountainbike Guide)
   Book 1:THE CAIRNGORM GLENS
   Book 2 THE ATHOLL GLENS
   Book 3 THE GLENS OF RANNOCH
SCOTTISH RAILWAY WALKS
SCRAMBLES IN LOCHABER
SCRAMBLES IN SKYE
SKI TOURING IN SCOTLAND
TORRIDON A Walker's Guide
WALKS from the WEST HIGHLAND RAILWAY
WINTER CLIMBS BEN NEVIS & GLENCOE

REGIONAL BOOKS UK & IRELAND
THE ALTERNATIVE PENNINE WAY
CANAL WALKS Vol.1: North
LIMESTONE - 100 BEST CLIMBS
THE PACKHORSE BRIDGES OF ENGLAND
THE RELATIVE HILLS OF BRITAIN
THE MOUNTAINS OF ENGLAND & WALES
   VOL 1 WALES, VOL 2 ENGLAND
THE MOUNTAINS OF IRELAND

Other guides are constantly being added to the Cicerone List.
Available from bookshops, outdoor equipment shops or direct (send s.a.e. for price list) from
CICERONE, 2 POLICE SQUARE, MILNTHORPE, CUMBRIA, LA7 7PY

Printed by CARNMOR PRINT & DESIGN
95-97 LONDON ROAD, PRESTON, LANCASHIRE, UK.